HERSHEY'S KISSES® BRAND

Recipes & Crafts

Publications International, Ltd.

© **2010 Publications International, Ltd.**

Recipes and text © 2010 The Hershey Company

Photographs on pages 19, 25, 34, 35, 38, 40, 41, 44, 45, 46, 57, 61, 62, 63, 66, 67, 81, 85, 90, 91, 93, 96, 99, 100, 101, 109, 111, 113, 115, 119, 120, 121, and 123 © The Hershey Company. All other photography © Publications International, Ltd.

Louis Weber, CEO
Publications International, Ltd.
7373 North Cicero Avenue
Lincolnwood, IL 60712

HERSHEY'S, HERSHEY'S Trade dress, KISSES, KISSES Conical Configuration and plume devise, HERSHEY-ETS, MINI KISSES, HUGS, BITS 'O BRICKLE, HERSHEY'S BLISS, HEATH, KIT KAT, MAUNA LOA, MOUNDS, POT OF GOLD, PULL N PEEL, REESE'S, REESE'S PIECES, ROLO, SPECIAL DARK, TWIZZLERS, TWIZZLERS NIBS are trademarks used under license.

Photography on pages 7, 31, 43, 49, 51, 55, 59, 65, 69, 73, 77, and 95 by PIL Photo Studio, Chicago, Il.

Photographer: Tate Hunt
Photographer's Assistant: Juan Palomino
Prop Stylist: Tom Hamilton
Food Stylists: Kim Hartman, Kathy Joy
Assistant Food Stylist: Brittany Culver

Photography on pages 103, 104, 105, 107, 108, 112, 116, and 117:

Craft Stylist: Jill Evans
Photographer: Christopher Hiltz

Pictured on the front cover (clockwise from top): KISSES Macaroon Cookies *(page 32)*, HUGS & KISSES Candy Box *(page 117)*, Tuxedo Torte *(page 68)* and HERSHEY'S KISSES Mice *(page 113)*.

Pictured on the back cover: Midnight Chocolate Cheesecake Cookie Cups *(page 58)*.

ISBN 13: 978-1-4508-0048-8
ISBN 10: 1-4508-0048-3

Manufactured in China.

8 7 6 5 4 3 2 1

Microwave Cooking: Microwave ovens vary in wattage. Use the cooking times as guidelines and check for doneness before adding more time.

# Contents

Classic
Favorites

MINI KISSES Blondies

Makes about 36 bars

1/2	cup (1 stick) butter or margarine, softened
11/3	cups packed light brown sugar
2	eggs
2	teaspoons vanilla extract
1/4	teaspoon salt
2	cups all-purpose flour
11/2	teaspoons baking powder
13/4	cups (10-ounce package) HERSHEY'S MINI KISSESBRAND Milk Chocolates
1/2	cup chopped nuts

1. Heat oven to 350°F. Lightly grease 13×9×2-inch baking pan.

2. Beat butter and brown sugar in large bowl until fluffy. Add eggs, vanilla and salt; beat until blended. Add flour and baking powder; beat just until blended. Stir in chocolate pieces. Spread batter in prepared pan. Sprinkle nuts over top.

3. Bake 28 to 30 minutes or until set and golden brown. Cool completely in pan on wire rack. Cut into bars.

REESE'S Peanut Butter & HERSHEY'S KISSES Pie

Makes 8 servings

About 42 HERSHEY'S KISSESBRAND **Milk Chocolates, divided**

2 **tablespoons milk**

1 **packaged (8-inch) crumb crust (6 ounces)**

1 **package (8 ounces) cream cheese, softened**

³/₄ **cup sugar**

1 **cup REESE'S Creamy Peanut Butter**

1 **container (8 ounces) frozen non-dairy whipped topping, thawed and divided**

1. Remove wrappers from chocolates. Place 26 chocolates and milk in small microwave-safe bowl. Microwave at MEDIUM (50%) 1 minute or just until melted and smooth when stirred. Spread evenly on bottom of crust. Refrigerate about 30 minutes.

2. Beat cream cheese with electric mixer on medium speed in medium bowl until smooth; gradually beat in sugar, then peanut butter, beating well after each addition. Reserve ¹/₂ cup whipped topping; fold remaining whipped topping into peanut butter mixture. Spoon into crust over chocolate. Cover; refrigerate about 6 hours or until set.

3. Garnish with reserved whipped topping and remaining chocolates. Cover; refrigerate leftover pie.

Thick and Fudgey Brownies with HERSHEY'S MINI KISSES Milk Chocolates

Makes 24 brownies

2¹/₄ cups all-purpose flour

²/₃ cup HERSHEY'S Cocoa

1 teaspoon baking powder

1 teaspoon salt

³/₄ cup (1¹/₂ sticks) butter or margarine, melted

2¹/₂ cups sugar

2 teaspoons vanilla extract

4 eggs

1³/₄ cups (10-ounce package) HERSHEY'S MINI KISSESBRAND Milk Chocolates

1. Heat oven to 350°F (325°F for glass baking dish). Grease 13×9×2-inch baking pan.

2. Stir together flour, cocoa, baking powder and salt. With spoon or whisk, stir together butter, sugar and vanilla in large bowl. Add eggs; stir until well blended. Stir in flour mixture, blending well. Stir in chocolate pieces. Spread batter in prepared pan.

3. Bake 30 to 35 minutes or until brownies begin to pull away from sides of pan. Cool completely in pan on wire rack; cut into 2-inch squares.

Peanut Butter Blossoms

Makes about 4 dozen cookies

48	HERSHEY'S KISSES BRAND Milk Chocolates
3/4	cup REESE'S Creamy Peanut Butter
1/2	cup shortening
1/3	cup granulated sugar
1/3	cup packed light brown sugar
1	egg
2	tablespoons milk
1	teaspoon vanilla extract
1 1/2	cups all-purpose flour
1	teaspoon baking soda
1/2	teaspoon salt
	Granulated sugar

1. Heat oven to 375°F. Remove wrappers from chocolates.

2. Beat peanut butter and shortening with electric mixer on medium speed in large bowl until well blended. Add 1/3 cup granulated sugar and brown sugar; beat until fluffy. Add egg, milk and vanilla; beat well. Stir together flour, baking soda and salt; gradually beat into peanut butter mixture.

3. Shape dough into 1-inch balls. Roll in additional granulated sugar; place on ungreased cookie sheet.

4. Bake 8 to 10 minutes or until lightly browned. Immediately press a chocolate into center of each cookie; cookies will crack around edges. Remove to wire racks and cool completely.

Fun Fact

In 1942, production of HERSHEY'S KISSES BRAND Chocolates were halted to save foil for the war effort.

HERSHEY'S Double Chocolate MINI KISSES Cookies

Makes about 3½ dozen cookies

1	cup (2 sticks) butter or margarine, softened
1½	cups sugar
2	eggs
2	teaspoons vanilla extract
2	cups all-purpose flour
²/₃	cup HERSHEY'S Cocoa
³/₄	teaspoon baking soda
¹/₄	teaspoon salt
1³/₄	cups (10-ounce package) HERSHEY'S MINI KISSES_{BRAND} Milk Chocolates
¹/₂	cup coarsely chopped nuts (optional)

1. Heat oven to 350°F.

2. Beat butter, sugar, eggs and vanilla with electric mixer on medium speed in large bowl until light and fluffy. Stir together flour, cocoa, baking soda and salt; add to butter mixture, beating until well blended. Stir in chocolates and nuts, if desired. Drop by tablespoons onto ungreased cookie sheet.

3. Bake 8 to 10 minutes or just until set. Cool slightly. Remove to wire rack and cool completely.

Rocky Road Tasty Team Treats

Makes about 36 bars

1½   cups finely crushed thin pretzels or pretzel sticks
¾   cup (1½ sticks) butter or margarine, melted
1   can (14 ounces) sweetened condensed milk (not evaporated milk)
1¾   cups (10-ounce package) HERSHEY'S MINI KISSES BRAND Milk Chocolates
3   cups miniature marshmallows
1⅓   cups coarsely chopped pecans or pecan pieces

1. Heat oven to 350°F. Grease bottom and sides of 13×9×2-inch baking pan.

2. Combine pretzels and melted butter in small bowl; press evenly onto bottom of prepared pan. Spread sweetened condensed milk evenly over pretzel layer; layer evenly with chocolates, marshmallows and pecans, in order. Press down firmly on pecans.

3. Bake 20 to 25 minutes or until lightly browned. Cool completely in pan on wire rack. Cut into bars.

Chocolate Magic Mousse Pie

1   envelope unflavored gelatin

2   tablespoons cold water

¹/₄   cup boiling water

1   cup sugar

¹/₂   cup HERSHEY'S Cocoa

2   cups (1 pint) cold whipping cream

2   teaspoons vanilla extract

1   packaged (8-inch) graham cracker crumb crust
    (6 ounces)

Refrigerated light whipped cream in pressurized can or frozen whipped topping, thawed

HERSHEY'S MINI KISSES BRAND Milk Chocolates

1. Sprinkle gelatin over cold water in small bowl; let stand 2 minutes to soften. Add boiling water; stir until gelatin is completely dissolved and mixture is clear. Cool slightly.

2. Mix sugar and cocoa in large bowl; add whipping cream and vanilla. Beat on medium speed, scraping bottom of bowl often, until mixture is stiff. Pour in gelatin mixture; beat until well blended.

3. Spoon into crust. Refrigerate about 3 hours. Garnish with whipped cream and chocolates. Cover; store leftover pie in refrigerator.

HERSHEY'S MINI KISSES Milk Chocolate Peanut Butter Cookies

Makes 1½ dozen cookies

- ¼ **cup (½ stick) butter or margarine, softened**
- ¼ **cup REESE'S Creamy Peanut Butter**
- ¼ **cup granulated sugar**
- ¼ **cup packed light brown sugar**
- 1 **egg**
- ½ **teaspoon vanilla extract**
- ⅔ **cup all-purpose flour**
- ¼ **teaspoon baking soda**
- ⅛ **teaspoon salt**
- 1¾ **cups (10-ounce package) HERSHEY'S MINI KISSES**BRAND **Milk Chocolates**

1. Heat oven to 350°F. Lightly grease cookie sheet.

2. Beat butter and peanut butter in large bowl on medium speed of electric mixer until creamy. Gradually add granulated sugar and brown sugar, beating until well mixed. Add egg and vanilla; beat until light and fluffy. Stir together flour, baking soda and salt; add to butter mixture, beating until well blended. Stir in chocolates. Drop batter by rounded tablespoons onto prepared cookie sheet.

3. Bake 10 to 12 minutes or until lightly browned. Cool slightly; remove from cookie sheet to wire rack. Cool completely.

Classic Favorites

HERSHEY'S Triple Chocolate Cookies

Makes about 4 dozen cookies

48   HERSHEY'S KISSESBRAND Milk Chocolates or HERSHEY'S KISSESBRAND Milk Chocolates with Almonds

1/2   cup (1 stick) butter or margarine, softened

3/4   cup granulated sugar

3/4   cup packed light brown sugar

1   teaspoon vanilla extract

2   eggs

1   tablespoon milk

2¹/4   cups all-purpose flour

1/3   cup HERSHEY'S Cocoa

1   teaspoon baking soda

1/2   teaspoon salt

1   cup HERSHEY'S SPECIAL DARK Chocolate Chips or HERSHEY'S Semi-Sweet Chocolate Chips

1. Remove wrappers from chocolates. Heat oven to 350°F.

2. Beat butter, granulated sugar, brown sugar and vanilla with electric mixer on medium speed in large bowl until well blended. Add eggs and milk; beat well.

3. Stir together flour, cocoa, baking soda and salt; gradually beat into butter mixture, beating until well blended. Stir in chocolate chips. Shape dough into 1-inch balls. Place on ungreased cookie sheet.

4. Bake 10 to 11 minutes or until set. Gently press a chocolate in center of each cookie. Remove to wire rack and cool completely.

Variation
For vanilla cookies, omit cocoa and add an additional 1/3 cup all-purpose flour.

Peanut Butter Cheesecake with Chocolate Drizzle

Makes 12 servings

1¼ cups graham cracker crumbs

⅓ cup plus ¼ cup sugar, divided

⅓ cup HERSHEY'S Cocoa

⅓ cup butter or margarine, melted

3 packages (8 ounces each) cream cheese, softened

1 can (14 ounces) sweetened condensed milk (not evaporated milk)

1⅔ cups (10-ounce package) REESE'S Peanut Butter Chips, melted

4 eggs

2 teaspoons vanilla extract

CHOCOLATE DRIZZLE (recipe follows)

Whipped topping

HERSHEY'S MINI KISSESBRAND Milk Chocolates

1. Heat oven to 300°F. Combine graham cracker crumbs, ⅓ cup sugar, cocoa and butter; press onto bottom of 9-inch springform pan.

2. Beat cream cheese and remaining ¼ cup sugar until fluffy. Gradually beat in sweetened condensed milk, then melted chips, until smooth. Add eggs and vanilla; beat well. Pour over crust.

3. Bake 60 to 70 minutes or until center is almost set. Remove from oven. With knife, loosen cake from side of pan. Cool. Remove side of pan. Refrigerate until cold. Garnish with CHOCOLATE DRIZZLE, whipped topping and chocolate

pieces. Store, covered, in refrigerator.

Chocolate Drizzle: Melt 2 tablespoons butter in small saucepan over low heat; add 2 tablespoons HERSHEY'S Cocoa and 2 tablespoons water.

Cook and stir until slightly thickened. Do not boil. Cool slightly. Gradually add 1 cup powdered sugar and 1/2 teaspoon vanilla extract, beating with whisk until smooth. Makes about 3/4 cup.

KISSES Chocolate Chip Cookies

Makes 4 dozen cookies

48 HERSHEY'S KISSESBRAND Milk Chocolates or HERSHEY'S KISSESBRAND Milk Chocolates with Almonds

1 cup (2 sticks) butter or margarine, softened

1/3 cup granulated sugar

1/3 cup packed light brown sugar

1 teaspoon vanilla extract

2 cups all-purpose flour

1 cup HERSHEY'S Mini Chips Semi-Sweet Chocolate

CHOCOLATE DRIZZLE (recipe follows)

1. Heat oven to 375°F. Remove wrappers from chocolates.

2. Beat butter, granulated sugar, brown sugar and vanilla in large bowl until well blended. Add flour to butter mixture; blend until smooth. Stir in small chocolate chips. Mold scant tablespoon dough around each chocolate, covering completely. Shape into balls; place on ungreased cookie sheet.

3. Bake 10 to 12 minutes or until set. Cool slightly; remove from cookie sheet to wire rack.

Cool completely. Prepare CHOCOLATE DRIZZLE; drizzle over each cookie.

Chocolate Drizzle: Place 1/4 cup HERSHEY'S Mini Chips Semi-Sweet Chocolate and 1 teaspoon shortening in small microwave-safe bowl. Microwave at MEDIUM (50%) 30 seconds; stir. If necessary, microwave at MEDIUM an additional 10 seconds at a time, stirring after each heating, until chocolate is melted and mixture is smooth when stirred.

Pecan MINI KISSES Cups

Makes 24 cups

- ½ cup (1 stick) butter or margarine, softened
- 1 package (3 ounces) cream cheese, softened
- 1 cup all-purpose flour
- 1 egg
- ⅔ cup packed light brown sugar
- 1 tablespoon butter, melted
- 1 teaspoon vanilla extract
- Dash salt
- 72 (about ½ cup) HERSHEY'S MINI KISSESʙʀᴀɴᴅ Milk Chocolates, divided
- ½ to ¾ cup coarsely chopped pecans

1. Beat ½ cup softened butter and cream cheese in medium bowl until blended. Add flour; beat well. Cover; refrigerate about 1 hour or until firm enough to handle.

2. Heat oven to 325°F. Stir together egg, brown sugar, 1 tablespoon melted butter, vanilla and salt in small bowl until well blended.

3. Shape chilled dough into 24 balls (1 inch each). Place balls in ungreased small muffin cups (1¾ inches in diameter). Press onto bottoms and up sides of cups. Place 2 chocolate pieces in each cup. Spoon about 1 teaspoon pecans over chocolate. Fill each cup with egg mixture.

4. Bake 25 minutes or until filling is set. Lightly press 1 chocolate into center of each cookie. Cool in pan on wire rack.

Tiny MINI KISSES Peanut Butter Blossoms

Makes about 14 dozen cookies

- ³/₄ **cup REESE'S Creamy Peanut Butter**
- ¹/₂ **cup shortening**
- ¹/₃ **cup granulated sugar**
- ¹/₃ **cup packed light brown sugar**
- 1 **egg**
- 3 **tablespoons milk**
- 1 **teaspoon vanilla extract**
- 1¹/₂ **cups all-purpose flour**
- ¹/₂ **teaspoon baking soda**
- ¹/₂ **teaspoon salt**
- **Granulated sugar**
- **HERSHEY'S MINI KISSES**BRAND **Milk Chocolates**

1. Heat oven to 350°F.

2. Beat peanut butter and shortening in large bowl with mixer until well blended. Add ¹/₃ cup granulated sugar and brown sugar; beat well. Add egg, milk and vanilla; beat until fluffy. Stir together flour, baking soda and salt; gradually add to peanut butter mixture, beating until blended. Shape into ¹/₂-inch balls. Roll in granulated sugar; place on ungreased cookie sheet.

3. Bake 5 to 6 minutes or until set. Immediately press chocolate into center of each cookie. Remove from cookie sheet to wire rack. Cool completely.

Variation: For larger cookies, shape dough into 1-inch balls. Roll in granulated sugar. Place on ungreased cookie sheet. Bake 10 minutes or until set. Immediately place 3 chocolate pieces in center of each cookie, pressing down slightly. Remove from cookie sheet to wire rack. Cool completely.

HERSHEY'S Double Chocolate Cheesecake

Makes about 20 squares or 10 to 12 wedges*

- ¹/₂ cup (1 stick) butter or margarine, softened
- 1¹/₄ cups sugar, divided
- ¹/₄ teaspoon salt
- 1 cup all-purpose flour
- ¹/₄ cup HERSHEY'S Cocoa
- 2 packages (8 ounces each) cream cheese, softened
- 2 eggs
- 2 teaspoons vanilla extract
- ¹/₂ cup HERSHEY'S Mini Chips Semi-Sweet Chocolate
- 18 HERSHEY'S KISSESBRAND Milk Chocolates
  Sweetened whipped cream (optional)
  Additional HERSHEY'S KISSESBRAND Milk Chocolates (optional)

1. Heat oven to 350°F. Line 8- or 9-inch square baking pan* with foil, extending edges over pan sides.

2. Beat butter, ¹/₂ cup sugar and salt in small bowl until smooth. Stir together flour and cocoa; gradually add to butter mixture, beating on low speed of mixer until soft dough is formed. Press dough onto bottom of prepared pan.

3. Beat cream cheese and remaining ³/₄ cup sugar in medium bowl until smooth. Add eggs and vanilla; beat until well blended. Remove 1 cup batter; set aside. Add small chocolate chips to remaining batter; pour over crust.

4. Remove wrappers from 18 chocolates; place in medium microwave-safe bowl. Microwave at MEDIUM (50%) 1 minute; stir. If necessary, microwave at MEDIUM an additional 15 seconds at a time, stirring after each heating, until chocolate is melted and smooth when stirred. Add to reserved batter, stirring until well blended. Drop by spoonfuls onto batter in pan; gently swirl with knife or spatula for marbled effect.

5. Bake 35 to 40 minutes or until cheesecake is firm and top is slightly puffed. Cool completely in pan on wire rack. Cover; refrigerate several hours until chilled. To serve, lift from pan using foil edges; cut into squares. Garnish each square with whipped cream and chocolate pieces, if desired. Cover; refrigerate leftover cheesecake.

*8- or 9-inch springform pan can also be used.

Variation
Sift together 1 tablespoon HERSHEY'S Cocoa with 1/3 cup powdered sugar. Roll warm cookies in cocoa mixture.

Secret KISSES Cookies

Makes 3 dozen cookies

- 1 cup (2 sticks) butter or margarine, softened
- 1/2 cup granulated sugar
- 1 teaspoon vanilla extract
- 1³/4 cups all-purpose flour
- 1 cup finely chopped walnuts or almonds
- 36 HERSHEY'S KISSES BRAND Milk Chocolates or HERSHEY'S KISSES BRAND Milk Chocolates with Almonds

Powdered sugar

1. Beat butter, granulated sugar and vanilla with electric mixer on medium speed in large bowl until fluffy. Add flour and walnuts; beat on low speed of mixer until well blended. Cover; refrigerate 1 to 2 hours or until dough is firm enough to handle.

2. Remove wrappers from chocolates. Heat oven to 375°F. Using about 1 tablespoon dough for each cookie, shape dough around each chocolate; roll in hand to make ball. (Be sure to cover each chocolate piece completely.) Place on ungreased cookie sheet.

3. Bake 10 to 12 minutes or until cookies are set but not browned. Cool slightly; remove to wire rack. While still slightly warm, roll in powdered sugar. Cool completely. Store in tightly covered container. Roll again in powdered sugar just before serving.

Marbled Peanut Butter Brownies

Makes about 36 brownies

- 2 packages (3 ounces each) cream cheese, softened
- 1/2 cup REESE'S Creamy Peanut Butter
- 2 1/4 cups sugar, divided
- 4 eggs
- 2 tablespoons milk
- 1 cup (2 sticks) butter or margarine
- 2 teaspoons vanilla extract
- 3/4 cup HERSHEY'S Cocoa
- 1 1/4 cups all-purpose flour
- 1/2 teaspoon baking powder
- 1/4 teaspoon salt
- 1 cup HERSHEY'S Milk Chocolate Chips or 1 cup HERSHEY'S MINI KISSES BRAND Milk Chocolates

1. Heat oven to 350°F. Grease 13×9×2-inch pan.

2. Prepare peanut butter filling by beating cream cheese, peanut butter, 1/4 cup sugar, 1 egg and milk.

3. Melt butter in large microwave-safe bowl at HIGH (100%) 2 to 2 1/2 minutes or until melted. Stir in remaining 2 cups sugar and vanilla. Add remaining 3 eggs, 1 at a time, beating well with spoon after each addition. Add cocoa; beat until well blended. Add flour, baking powder and salt; beat well. Stir in chocolate chips.

4. Remove 1 cup batter; set aside. Pour remaining batter into prepared pan. Spread peanut butter filling over surface. Drop reserved chocolate batter by teaspoons over filling. Using knife, gently swirl through top layers for marbled effect.

5. Bake 35 to 40 minutes or until wooden pick inserted in center comes out almost clean. Cool completely in pan or wire rack. Cut into bars.

Cappuccino-KISSed Cheesecake

Makes 16 servings

1½	cups chocolate cookie crumbs
6	tablespoons butter or margarine, melted
1¼	cups HERSHEY'S MINI KISSESBRAND Milk Chocolates, divided
4	packages (8 ounces each) cream cheese, softened
⅔	cup sugar
3	eggs
⅓	cup milk
1	tablespoon instant espresso powder
¼	teaspoon ground cinnamon
	ESPRESSO CREAM (recipe follows)

1. Heat oven to 350°F. Combine cookie crumbs and butter; press onto bottom and 1 inch up side of 9-inch springform pan.

2. Melt 1 cup chocolate pieces in small saucepan over low heat, stirring constantly. Combine cream cheese and sugar in large bowl, beating on medium speed of mixer until well blended. Add eggs, milk, espresso powder and cinnamon; beat on low speed until well blended. Add melted chocolate pieces; beat on medium 2 minutes. Spoon mixture into crust.

3. Bake 55 minutes. Remove from oven to wire rack. Cool 15 minutes; with knife, loosen cake from side of pan. Cool completely; remove side of pan. Cover; refrigerate at least 4 hours before serving.

4. To serve, garnish with ESPRESSO CREAM and remaining ¼ cup chocolates. Cover; refrigerate leftover cheesecake.

Espresso Cream: Beat ½ cup cold whipping cream, 2 tablespoons powdered sugar and 1 teaspoon instant espresso powder until stiff.

Fun Fact

It takes approximately 95 HERSHEY'S KISSESBRAND Chocolates to equal 1 pound of chocolate.

Classic MINI KISSES Cookie Mix (Cookie Mix in a Jar)

Makes 1 jar mix

- $2^{1}/_{4}$ cups all-purpose flour
- $^{2}/_{3}$ cup granulated sugar
- 1 teaspoon baking soda
- $^{1}/_{2}$ teaspoon salt
- $1^{1}/_{2}$ cups HERSHEY'S MINI KISSESBRAND Milk Chocolates, divided
- $^{2}/_{3}$ cup packed light brown sugar
- BAKING INSTRUCTIONS (recipe follows)

1. Stir together flour, granulated sugar, baking soda and salt. Transfer mixture to clean 1-quart (4 cups) glass jar with lid; pack down into bottom of jar.

2. Layer with 1 cup chocolate pieces and brown sugar.* Top with remaining $^{1}/_{2}$ cup chocolates; close jar. Attach card with BAKING INSTRUCTIONS.

To increase shelf life of mix, wrap brown sugar in plastic wrap and press into place.

Classic MINI KISSES Cookies

Makes 3 dozen cookies

- 1 jar Classic MINI KISSESBRAND Cookie Mix
- 1 cup (2 sticks) butter, softened and cut into pieces
- 1 teaspoon vanilla extract
- 2 eggs, lightly beaten

BAKING INSTRUCTIONS:

1. Heat oven to 375°F.

2. Spoon contents of jar into large bowl; stir to break up any lumps. Add butter and vanilla extract; stir until crumbly mixture forms. Add eggs; stir to form smooth, very stiff dough. Drop by heaping teaspoons onto ungreased cookie sheet.

3. Bake 8 to 10 minutes or until lightly browned. Cool slightly; remove from cookie sheet to wire rack. Cool completely.

Tip

For best results, use cookie mix within 4 weeks of assembly.

Bite-Size Treats

Chocolate Almond Thumbprint Cookies

Makes about 3½ dozen cookies

- 1 cup (2 sticks) butter or margarine, softened
- 2/3 cup sugar
- 2 egg yolks
- 1/2 teaspoon vanilla extract
- 2 cups all-purpose flour
- 1/4 cup HERSHEY'S Cocoa
- 1/2 teaspoon salt
- 1 cup finely chopped almonds
- CHOCOLATE FILLING (recipe follows)
- 42 HERSHEY'S KISSES BRAND Milk Chocolates with Almonds

1. Heat oven to 350°F. Beat butter, sugar, egg yolks and vanilla until well blended. Stir together flour, cocoa and salt; gradually beat into butter mixture.

2. Roll dough into 1-inch balls; roll balls in almonds. Place on ungreased cookie sheet. Press thumb gently in center of each cookie.

3. Bake 18 to 20 minutes or until set. Remove from cookie sheet to wire rack. Cool completely.

4. Prepare CHOCOLATE FILLING. Remove wrappers from chocolates. Spoon or pipe about 1/4 teaspoon filling into each thumbprint. Gently press candy in center of each cookie.

Chocolate Filling: Combine 1/2 cup powdered sugar, 1 tablespoon HERSHEY'S Cocoa, 1 tablespoon softened butter, 2½ teaspoons milk and 1/4 teaspoon vanilla extract in small bowl; beat until smooth.

KISSES Macaroon Cookies

Makes about 4 dozen cookies

⅓	cup butter or margarine, softened
1	package (3 ounces) cream cheese, softened
¾	cup sugar
1	egg yolk
2	teaspoons almond extract
2	teaspoons orange juice
1¼	cups all-purpose flour
2	teaspoons baking powder
¼	teaspoon salt
5	cups MOUNDS Sweetened Coconut Flakes, divided
48	HERSHEY'S KISSESʙʀᴀɴᴅ Milk Chocolates

1. Beat butter, cream cheese and sugar with electric mixer on medium speed in large bowl until well blended. Add egg yolk, almond extract and orange juice; beat well. Stir together flour, baking powder and salt; gradually add to butter mixture. Stir in 3 cups coconut. Cover; refrigerate 1 hour or until firm enough to handle. Meanwhile, remove wrappers from chocolates.

2. Heat oven to 350°F.

3. Shape dough into 1-inch balls; roll in remaining 2 cups coconut. Place on ungreased cookie sheet.

4. Bake 10 to 12 minutes or until lightly browned. Immediately press chocolate piece into center of each cookie. Cool 1 minute. Carefully remove to wire rack and cool completely.

MINI KISSES Fruit Bars

Makes 36 bars

1½ cups all-purpose flour

1½ cups quick-cooking rolled oats

1 cup packed light brown sugar

1 teaspoon baking powder

¾ cup (1½ sticks) butter or margarine, softened

1 jar (10 to 12 ounces) raspberry jam

1¾ cups (10-ounce package) HERSHEY'S MINI KISSES BRAND Milk Chocolates

½ cup chopped nuts (optional)

1. Heat oven to 350°F. Lightly grease 13×9×2-inch baking pan.

2. Combine flour, oats, brown sugar and baking powder in large bowl. Cut butter into flour mixture with pastry blender or two knives until crumbly. Remove 2 cups crumb mixture; set aside.

3. Press remaining crumb mixture onto bottom of prepared pan. Stir jam to soften; carefully spread over crumb mixture. Sprinkle chocolates evenly over jam. Cover with reserved crumbs. Sprinkle nuts over top, if desired; press firmly.

4. Bake 40 to 45 minutes or until lightly browned. Cool completely in pan on wire rack. Cut into bars.

Caramel Nut Bundles

Makes 8 pastry bundles

20 HERSHEY'S KISSES_{BRAND} Milk Chocolates filled with Caramel

1 can (8 ounces) refrigerated quick crescent dinner rolls

1 tablespoon butter or margarine, melted

$^1/_4$ cup pecan, walnut or peanut pieces

$^3/_4$ teaspoon water

1. Heat oven to 375°F. Remove wrappers from chocolates. Unroll dough; separate into 8 triangles.

2. Spread melted butter on each triangle. Place 2 chocolates at wide end of each triangle; sprinkle with about 1 teaspoon nut pieces. Take dough on one side of wide end and pull up and over chocolate pieces, tucking under chocolates and nuts. Pull dough from remaining side up and over chocolates and dough, tucking under. Continue rolling pastry covered chocolates toward opposite point. Place rolls on ungreased cookie sheet with smooth side up.

3. Bake 10 minutes or until lightly browned. Meanwhile place remaining chocolates and water in small microwave-safe bowl. Microwave at MEDIUM (50%) 30 seconds; stir. If necessary, microwave at MEDIUM an additional 10 seconds at a time, stirring after each heating, until chocolates are melted and mixture is smooth when stirred. Drizzle over warm pastries. Serve warm.

Cookie Trio

Makes about 4 dozen cookies

- ¹/₂ **cup (1 stick) butter or margarine, softened**
- ¹/₂ **cup shortening**
- 1 **cup sugar**
- 1 **egg**
- 1 **teaspoon vanilla extract**
- 2 **cups plus 2 tablespoons all-purpose flour, divided**
- 1 **teaspoon baking powder**
- ¹/₄ **teaspoon salt**
- 2 **tablespoons HERSHEY'S SPECIAL DARK Cocoa**
- 48 **HERSHEY'S HUGS**BRAND **Candies**

1. Heat oven to 350°F.

2. Beat butter, shortening and sugar until well blended. Beat in egg and vanilla. Stir together 2 cups flour, baking powder and salt. Gradually beat into butter mixture.

3. Divide dough mixture into halves. Add remaining 2 tablespoons flour to one half and cocoa to the other half, blending well. Roll dough into 1-inch balls. (Roll together a pinch of vanilla dough and a pinch of chocolate dough for marbled cookies.)

Place balls on ungreased cookie sheets.

4. Bake 9 to 11 minutes or until cookies are set. Remove from oven to wire rack. Cool 1 minute. Press candy piece into center of each cookie. Remove from cookie sheets to wire rack; cool completely.

Cheery Cheesecake Cookie Bars

Makes 36 bars

1   package (4 ounces) HERSHEY'S Unsweetened Chocolate Baking Bar, broken into pieces

1   cup (2 sticks) butter

2¹/₂   cups sugar, divided

4   eggs

1   teaspoon vanilla extract

2   cups all-purpose flour

1   package (8 ounces) cream cheese, softened

1³/₄   cups (10-ounce package) HERSHEY'S MINI KISSESʙʀᴀɴᴅ Milk Chocolates, divided

¹/₂   cup chopped red or green maraschino cherries

¹/₂   teaspoon almond extract

     Few drops red food color (optional)

1. Heat oven to 350°F. Grease 13×9×2-inch baking pan.

2. Place unsweetened chocolate and butter in large microwave-safe bowl. Microwave at MEDIUM (50%) 2 to 2¹/₂ minutes, stirring after each minute, until mixture is melted. Beat in 2 cups sugar, 3 eggs and vanilla until blended. Stir in flour; spread batter in prepared pan.

3. Beat cream cheese, remaining ¹/₂ cup sugar and remaining 1 egg; stir in 1¹/₄ cups chocolate pieces, cherries, almond extract and red food color, if desired. Drop by spoonfuls over top of chocolate mixture in pan.

4. Bake 35 to 40 minutes or just until set. Remove from oven; immediately sprinkle remaining ¹/₂ cup chocolates over top. Cool completely in pan on wire rack; cut into bars. Cover; refrigerate leftover bars.

Fudgey Coconut Clusters

Makes about 2½ dozen cookies

5⅓   **cups MOUNDS Sweetened Coconut Flakes**

1   **can (14 ounces) sweetened condensed milk (not evaporated milk)**

⅔   **cup HERSHEY'S Cocoa**

¼   **cup (½ stick) butter or margarine, melted**

2   **teaspoons vanilla extract**

1½   **teaspoons almond extract**

  HERSHEY'S MINI KISSESBRAND **Milk Chocolates or candied cherry halves (optional)**

1. Heat oven to 350°F. Line cookie sheets with aluminum foil; generously grease foil with vegetable shortening.

2. Combine coconut, sweetened condensed milk, cocoa, melted butter, vanilla and almond extract in large bowl; mix well. Drop by rounded tablespoons onto prepared cookie sheets.

3. Bake 9 to 11 minutes or just until set; press 3 milk chocolates or candied cherry halves in center of each cookie, if desired. Immediately remove cookies to wire racks and cool completely.

Chocolate Chip Macaroons: Omit cocoa and melted butter; stir together other ingredients. Add 1 cup HERSHEY'S Mini Chips Semi-Sweet Chocolate. Bake 9 to 11 minutes or just until set. Immediately remove to wire racks and cool completely.

Chocolate Thumbprint Cookies

Makes about 2 dozen cookies

1/2   cup (1 stick) butter or margarine, softened

2/3   cup sugar

  1   egg, separated

  2   tablespoons milk

  1   teaspoon vanilla extract

  1   cup all-purpose flour

1/3   cup HERSHEY'S Cocoa

1/4   teaspoon salt

  1   cup chopped nuts

       VANILLA FILLING (recipe follows)

 26   HERSHEY'S KISSESBRAND Milk Chocolates, HERSHEY'S HUGSBRAND Candies, pecan halves or candied cherry halves

1. Beat butter, sugar, egg yolk, milk and vanilla in medium bowl until fluffy. Stir together flour, cocoa and salt; gradually add to butter mixture, beating until blended. Refrigerate dough at least 1 hour or until firm enough to handle.

2. Heat oven to 350°F. Lightly grease cookie sheet. Shape dough into 1-inch balls. With fork, beat egg white slightly. Dip each ball into egg white; roll in nuts. Place on prepared cookie sheet. Press thumb gently in center of each cookie.

3. Bake cookies 10 to 12 minutes or until set. Meanwhile, prepare VANILLA FILLING. Remove wrappers from chocolate pieces. Remove cookies from cookie sheet to wire rack; cool 5 minutes. Spoon about 1/4 teaspoon prepared filling into each thumbprint. Gently press chocolate piece onto top of each cookie. Cool completely.

VANILLA FILLING: Combine 1/2 cup powdered sugar, 1 tablespoon softened butter or margarine, 2 teaspoons milk and 1/4 teaspoon vanilla extract in small bowl; beat until smooth.

Variation: Omit egg white and chopped nuts. Roll balls in granulated sugar. Bake as directed. Top with VANILLA FILLING and pecan or cherry half.

Cherry Cordial Chocolate Thumbprint Cookies: Substitute HERSHEY'S KISSESBRAND Milk Chocolates filled with Cherry Cordial Crème or HERSHEY'S KISSESBRAND Dark Chocolates filled with Cherry Cordial Crème for the HERSHEY'S KISSESBRAND Milk Chocolates or HERSHEY'S HUGSBRAND Candies.

Krunchy KISSES Cookies

Makes about 3 dozen cookies

- 36 **HERSHEY'S KISSESBRAND Milk Chocolates**
- 1/2 **cup light corn syrup**
- 1/4 **cup packed light brown sugar**
- 1 **cup REESE'S Creamy Peanut Butter**
- 1 **teaspoon vanilla extract**
- 2 **cups crisp rice cereal**
- 1 **cup slightly crushed corn flakes**

1. Remove wrappers from chocolate pieces.

2. Stir together corn syrup and brown sugar in medium saucepan. Cook over medium heat, stirring constantly, until mixture comes to full boil. Remove from heat; stir in peanut butter and vanilla. Add cereals; stir until well coated.

3. Drop by teaspoons onto ungreased cookie sheet. Loosely shape into balls; gently press chocolate piece in center of each ball, shaping ball gently into cookie shape. Store in covered container at room temperature.

Tuxedo Brownie HUGS Cookies

Makes about 5 dozen cookies

60 HERSHEY'S HUGSBRAND Candies

1 family size (13×9-inch pan) original supreme brownie mix with HERSHEY'S Syrup Pouch

1/4 cup HERSHEY'S Cocoa

1/4 cup water

1/4 cup vegetable oil

2 eggs

1. Remove wrappers from candies. Heat oven to 350°F. Grease and flour cookie sheet or line with parchment paper.

2. Stir brownie mix, pouch of HERSHEY'S Syrup, cocoa, water, oil and eggs in medium bowl until well blended. Drop by scant teaspoons onto prepared cookie sheet.

3. Bake 8 minutes or until set. Cool 1 minute. Press candy into center of each cookie. Remove from cookie sheet to wire rack. Cool completely.

Cherry Cordial Crème Cookies: Substitute HERSHEY'S KISSESBRAND Milk Chocolates filled with Cherry Cordial Crème or HERSHEY'S KISSESBRAND Dark Chocolates filled with Cherry Cordial Crème for the HERSHEY'S HUGSBRAND Candies.

Double Chocolate KISSES Cookies

Makes about 3 dozen cookies

½ cup (1 stick) butter or margarine, softened

1 cup sugar

1 egg

1½ teaspoons vanilla extract

1½ cups all-purpose flour

⅓ cup HERSHEY'S Cocoa

½ teaspoon baking soda

¼ teaspoon salt

¼ cup milk

36 HERSHEY'S KISSESBRAND Milk Chocolates or HERSHEY'S HUGSBRAND Candies

1 can (16 ounces) vanilla ready-to-spread frosting

1. Beat butter, sugar, egg and vanilla in large bowl until well blended. Add flour, cocoa, baking soda and salt alternately with milk, beating until well blended. Cover; refrigerate dough about 1 hour or until firm enough to handle. Shape dough into 1-inch balls; place on ungreased cookie sheet.

2. Heat oven to 375°F. Remove wrappers from chocolate pieces.

3. Bake 8 to 10 minutes or until set. Cool 1 minute; remove from cookie sheet to wire rack. Cool completely. Spread frosting onto cookies, leaving about ½ inch around outer edge unfrosted; place chocolate piece in center of each cookie.

Butter-Nut Chocolate Topped Cookies

Makes about 2½ dozen cookies

- ½ cup (1 stick) butter or margarine, softened
- ½ cup sugar
- 1 egg
- 1 teaspoon vanilla extract
- 1¼ cups all-purpose flour
- ¼ teaspoon baking soda
- ⅛ teaspoon salt
- 30 HERSHEY'S KISSESBRAND Milk Chocolates
- ½ cup ground almonds, pecans or walnuts

1. Beat butter, sugar, egg and vanilla in medium bowl until well blended. Stir together flour, baking soda and salt; add to butter mixture, beating well. If necessary, refrigerate dough until firm enough to handle.

2. Remove wrappers from chocolates. Heat oven to 350°F. Shape dough into 1-inch balls; roll in ground nuts. Place on ungreased cookie sheet.

3. Bake 10 to 12 minutes or until almost no imprint remains when touched lightly in center. Remove from oven;

immediately press a chocolate into center of each cookie. Carefully remove from cookie sheet to wire rack. Cool completely. Chocolate should be set before storing.

Orange Variation: Add ¾ teaspoon freshly grated orange peel to butter mixture.

Fun Fact

Hershey makes more than 80 million HERSHEY'S KISSESBRAND Chocolates every day.

Chocolate Meltaway Brownie Bites

- **48 HERSHEY'S KISSES**BRAND **Chocolate Meltaway Milk Chocolates**
- **2/3 cup butter or margarine, softened**
- **1¼ cups granulated sugar**
- **1 tablespoon water**
- **1 teaspoon vanilla extract**
- **2 eggs**
- **1½ cups all-purpose flour**
- **½ cup HERSHEY'S Cocoa or HERSHEY'S SPECIAL DARK Cocoa**
- **½ teaspoon salt**
- **¼ teaspoon baking soda**
- **Powdered sugar**

1. Remove wrappers from chocolates; place in freezer while preparing and baking cookies.

2. Beat butter, granulated sugar, water and vanilla in large bowl on medium speed of mixer until well blended. Add eggs; beat well. Stir together flour, cocoa, salt and baking soda. Gradually add to sugar mixture, beating on low speed until blended. Cover; refrigerate dough about two hours or until firm enough to handle.

3. Heat oven to 350°F. Line 48 small muffin cups (1¾ inches in diameter) with paper or foil baking cups or lightly spray with vegetable cooking spray. Shape dough into 1-inch balls; place in prepared muffin cups.

4. Bake 11 to 13 minutes or until cookie surface is set. Cookies will appear soft and moist. Do not overbake. Cool about 5 minutes on wire rack. Dust cookie tops with powdered sugar. Press frozen chocolate piece into surface of each cookie. Cool completely in pan on wire rack.

KISSed Pretzel S'mores

Make as desired

Small pretzels (twisted)
Miniature marshmallows
HERSHEY'S KISSESBRAND **Milk Chocolates**

1. Heat oven to 350°F. Line cookie sheet with parchment paper or foil.

2. Place one pretzel for each pretzel's s'more desired on prepared sheet. Top each pretzel with 3 marshmallows and another pretzel.

3. Bake 4 to 5 minutes or until marshmallows soften and begin to puff. Remove from oven and gently press chocolate on each top pretzel. Allow treats to sit several minutes in order for chocolate pieces to melt enough to adhere to pretzels and to soften slightly. Treats are best if eaten while chocolate piece is soft.

Chocolate Dipped Toffee Bits Cookies

Makes 4 dozen cookies

2¹/₄ cups all-purpose flour

1 teaspoon baking soda

¹/₂ teaspoon salt

¹/₂ cup (1 stick) butter or margarine, softened

³/₄ cup granulated sugar

³/₄ cup packed light brown sugar

1 teaspoon vanilla extract

2 eggs

1¹/₃ cups (8-ounce package) HEATH BITS 'O BRICKLE Toffee Bits

1³/₄ cups (10-ounce package) HERSHEY'S MINI KISSESBRAND Milk Chocolates

2 tablespoons shortening (do not use butter, margarine, spread or oil)

1. Heat oven to 350°F. Lightly grease cookie sheet.

2. Stir together flour, baking soda and salt; set aside. Beat butter, granulated sugar, brown sugar and vanilla in large bowl until well blended. Add eggs; beat well. Gradually add flour mixture, beating until well blended. Stir in toffee bits. Drop by rounded teaspoons onto prepared cookie sheet.

3. Bake 9 to 11 minutes or until lightly browned. Cool slightly; remove from cookie sheet to wire rack. Cool completely.

4. Line tray with wax paper. Place chocolates and shortening in medium, microwave-safe bowl. Microwave at MEDIUM (50%) 1 minute; stir. If necessary, microwave at MEDIUM an additional 15 seconds at a time, stirring

after each heating, until chocolates are melted and mixture is smooth when stirred.

5. Dip about one-half of each cookie into melted chocolate. Shake gently and scrape cookie bottom on edge of bowl to remove excess chocolate. Place on prepared tray. Refrigerate until chocolate is firm, about 30 minutes. Store in cool, dry place with wax paper between layers of cookies.

Caramel Thumbprint Cookies

Makes 4 dozen cookies

66 **HERSHEY'S KISSES**BRAND **Milk Chocolates filled with Caramel**

1 **family size (13×9-inch pan) original supreme brownie mix with HERSHEY'S Syrup Pouch**

1/4 **cup HERSHEY'S Cocoa**

2 **eggs**

1 **tablespoon vegetable oil**

1 **tablespoon water**

1 **cup ground pecans (optional)**

2 **teaspoons milk**

1. Remove wrappers from caramel filled chocolates. Lightly grease cookie sheets.

2. Beat brownie mix, pouch of syrup, cocoa, eggs, oil and water in medium bowl until well blended. Cover; refrigerate about 1 hour or until thoroughly chilled (dough will still be sticky).

3. Heat oven to 350°F. Shape dough into 48 (1-inch) balls. (Return dough to refrigerator if necessary or drop by rounded teaspoons onto wax paper-lined trays and refrigerate about 10 minutes.) Roll balls in pecans, if desired. Place on prepared cookie sheets; press thumb gently in center of each cookie. Bake 9 to 11 minutes or until set. Cool slightly; remove from cookie sheets to wire rack. Cool completely.

4. Place 18 caramel filled chocolates and milk in small microwave-safe bowl. Microwave at MEDIUM (50%) 30 seconds; stir. If necessary, microwave at MEDIUM an additional 10 seconds at a time, stirring after each heating, until chocolates are melted and smooth when stirred. Spoon slightly rounded 1/4 teaspoon caramel mixture into center of each cookie. Lightly press chocolate in center of each cookie.

Chunky Macadamia Bars

Makes 24 bars

- ³/₄ cup (1¹/₂ sticks) butter or margarine, softened
- 1 cup packed light brown sugar
- ¹/₂ cup granulated sugar
- 1 egg
- 1 teaspoon vanilla extract
- 2¹/₄ cups all-purpose flour
- 1 teaspoon baking soda
- 1³/₄ cups (10-ounce package) HERSHEY'S MINI KISSESBRAND Milk Chocolates, divided
- ³/₄ cup MAUNA LOA Macadamia Baking Pieces
- VANILLA GLAZE (recipe follows)

1. Heat oven to 375°F.

2. Beat butter, brown sugar and granulated sugar in large bowl until fluffy. Add egg and vanilla; beat well. Add flour and baking soda; blend well. Stir in 1 cup chocolate pieces and nuts; press into ungreased 13×9×2-inch baking pan. Sprinkle with remaining ³/₄ cup chocolates.

3. Bake 22 to 25 minutes or until golden brown. Cool completely in pan on wire rack. Drizzle VANILLA GLAZE over top; allow to set. Cut into bars.

Vanilla Glaze: Combine 1 cup powdered sugar, 2 tablespoons milk and ¹/₂ teaspoon vanilla extract in small bowl; stir until smooth. Makes ¹/₃ cup glaze.

MINI KISSES Butter Pecan Bars

Makes about 16 bars

- ¹/₂ **cup (1 stick) butter, softened**
- ¹/₂ **cup packed light brown sugar**
- 1 **egg**
- 1 **teaspoon vanilla extract**
- ³/₄ **cup all-purpose flour**
- 1³/₄ **cups (10-ounce package) HERSHEY'S MINI KISSES**BRAND **Milk Chocolates, divided**
- ³/₄ **cup coarsely chopped pecans, divided**

1. Heat oven to 350°F. Grease 8-inch square baking pan.

2. Beat butter, brown sugar, egg and vanilla in medium bowl; blend in flour. Stir in ³/₄ cup chocolates and ¹/₄ cup pecans; spread evenly in prepared pan.

3. Bake 25 to 30 minutes or until lightly browned; remove from oven. Immediately sprinkle remaining 1 cup chocolate pieces over top. Let stand 5 minutes or until chocolate softens; with knife, spread evenly. Immediately sprinkle remaining ¹/₂ cup pecans over top; press gently. Cool completely in pan on wire rack. Cut into bars.

KISSES Cocoa Cookies

Makes about 4½ dozen cookies

1 cup (2 sticks) butter or margarine, softened

²/₃ cup granulated sugar

1 teaspoon vanilla extract

1²/₃ cups all-purpose flour

¼ cup HERSHEY'S Cocoa

1 cup finely chopped pecans

About 54 HERSHEY'S KISSESʙʀᴀɴᴅ Milk Chocolates

Powdered sugar

1. Beat butter, granulated sugar and vanilla in large bowl until creamy. Stir together flour and cocoa; gradually add to butter mixture, beating until well blended. Add pecans; beat until well blended. Refrigerate dough about 1 hour or until firm enough to handle.

2. Heat oven to 375°F. Remove wrappers from chocolate pieces. Mold scant tablespoon of dough around each chocolate piece, covering completely. Shape into balls. Place on ungreased cookie sheet.

3. Bake 10 to 12 minutes or until set. Cool about 1 minute; remove from cookie sheet to wire rack. Cool completely. Roll in powdered sugar. Roll in powdered sugar again just before serving, if desired.

Fun Fact
The street lamps in Hershey, PA are shaped like HERSHEY'S KISSESʙʀᴀɴᴅ Chocolates.

California Chocolate Bars

Makes about 16 bars

6   tablespoons butter or margarine, softened
1/2 cup granulated sugar
1/4 cup packed light brown sugar
1   egg
1   teaspoon freshly grated orange peel
1   teaspoon vanilla extract
1   cup all-purpose flour
1/2 teaspoon baking soda
1/4 teaspoon salt
1/2 cup chopped dried apricots
1/2 cup coarsely chopped walnuts
1   cup HERSHEY'S MINI KISSESBRAND Milk Chocolates
    MILK CHOCOLATE GLAZE (recipe follows, optional)

1. Heat oven to 350°F. Grease 9-inch square baking pan.

2. Beat butter, granulated sugar, brown sugar and egg in large bowl until fluffy. Add orange peel and vanilla; beat until blended. Stir together flour, baking soda and salt; add to orange mixture. Stir in apricots, walnuts and chocolates; spread in prepared pan.

3. Bake 25 to 30 minutes or until lightly browned and bars begin to pull away from sides of pan. Cool completely in pan on wire rack. Prepare MILK CHOCOLATE GLAZE, if desired; drizzle over top. Allow to set; cut into bars.

Milk Chocolate Glaze: Place 1/4 cup HERSHEY'S MINI KISSESBRAND Milk Chocolates and 3/4 teaspoon shortening (do not use butter, margarine, spread or oil) in small microwave-safe bowl. Microwave at MEDIUM (50%) 45 seconds or until chocolates are melted and mixture is smooth when stirred.

Quarterback Blitz Bars

Makes about 36 bars

- 1 **cup (2 sticks) butter or margarine**
- 2¼ **cups graham cracker crumbs**
- ⅓ **cup HERSHEY'S Cocoa**
- 3 **tablespoons sugar**
- 1 **can (14 ounces) sweetened condensed milk (not evaporated milk)**
- 1 **cup HERSHEY'S MINI KISSES**BRAND **Milk Chocolates**
- 1 **cup HEATH BITS 'O BRICKLE Toffee Bits**
- 1 **cup chopped walnuts**
- 1 **cup MOUNDS Sweetened Coconut Flakes**

1. Heat oven to 350°F. Place butter in 13×9×2-inch baking pan; heat in oven until melted. Remove from oven.

2. Stir together graham cracker crumbs, cocoa and sugar; sprinkle over melted butter. Stir mixture until evenly coated; press evenly with spatula onto bottom of pan. Pour sweetened condensed milk evenly over crumb mixture. Sprinkle with chocolate pieces and toffee bits. Sprinkle nuts and coconut on top; press down firmly.

3. Bake 25 to 30 minutes or until lightly browned. Cool completely in pan on wire rack. Cover with foil; let stand at room temperature several hours. Cut into bars.

Pies, Cakes and More

Easy MINI KISSES Choco-Cherry Pie

Makes about 8 servings

1	baked (9-inch) pie crust, cooled
1³/₄	cups (10-ounce package) HERSHEY'S MINI KISSES BRAND Milk Chocolates, divided
1¹/₂	cups miniature marshmallows
¹/₃	cup milk
1	cup (¹/₂ pint) cold whipping cream
1	can (21 ounces) cherry pie filling, chilled
	Whipped topping

1. Prepare pie crust.

2. Place 1 cup chocolate pieces, marshmallows and milk in medium microwave-safe bowl. Microwave at MEDIUM (50%) 1¹/₂ to 2 minutes or until chocolate is softened and mixture is melted and smooth when stirred; cool completely.

3. Beat whipping cream in small bowl until stiff; fold into chocolate mixture. Spoon into prepared crust. Cover; refrigerate 4 hours or until firm.

4. Garnish top of pie with cherry pie filling, whipped topping and remaining chocolates just before serving. Refrigerate leftover pie.

KISSES Fluted Cups with Peanut Butter Filling

Makes about 2 dozen pieces

72   HERSHEY'S KISSES_{BRAND} Milk Chocolates, divided
1   cup REESE'S Creamy Peanut Butter
1   cup powdered sugar
1   tablespoon butter or margarine, softened

1. Line 24 small muffin cups (1³⁄₄ inches in diameter) with small paper bake cups. Remove wrappers from chocolates.

2. Place 48 chocolates in small microwave-safe bowl. Microwave at MEDIUM (50%) 1 minute; stir. Microwave at MEDIUM an additional 10 seconds at a time, stirring after each heating, just until chocolate is melted when stirred. Using small brush, coat inside of paper cups with melted chocolate.

3. Refrigerate 20 minutes; reapply melted chocolate to any thin spots. Refrigerate until firm, preferably overnight. Gently peel paper from chocolate cups.

4. Beat peanut butter, powdered sugar and butter with electric mixer on medium speed in small bowl until smooth. Spoon into chocolate cups. Before serving, top each cup with a chocolate piece. Cover; store cups in refrigerator.

Double KISSES Truffles

Makes 10 truffles

28 HERSHEY'S KISSESBRAND Milk Chocolates*

2 tablespoons plus 2 teaspoons heavy cream

10 HERSHEY'S KISSESBRAND Milk Chocolates filled with Caramel

1 cup ground pecans

³/₄ cup HERSHEY'S MINI KISSESBRAND Milk Chocolates may be substituted for HERSHEY'S KISSESBRAND Milk Chocolates.

1. Remove wrappers from milk chocolates. Place milk chocolates and heavy cream in medium microwave-safe bowl. Microwave at MEDIUM (50%) 1 minute; stir. If necessary, microwave at MEDIUM 15 seconds at a time, stirring after each heating, until chocolates are melted and mixture is smooth when stirred. Cover; refrigerate 4 to 6 hours or until firm.

2. Remove wrappers from caramel filled milk chocolates.

Mold about 1 tablespoon milk chocolate mixture around each caramel chocolate piece; roll in hand to make ball. (Be sure to cover each chocolate piece completely.) Roll in pecans; refrigerate until ready to serve. For best chocolate flavor, allow truffles to soften at room temperature about 5 minutes before eating.

Note Recipe may be multiplied.

Midnight Chocolate Cheesecake Cookie Cups

Makes 30 dessert cups

- $1/4$ cup ($1/2$ stick) butter, softened
- $1/4$ cup shortening
- $1/2$ cup sugar
- 1 egg
- $1/2$ teaspoon vanilla extract
- 1 cup all-purpose flour
- 2 tablespoons HERSHEY'S SPECIAL DARK Cocoa or HERSHEY'S Cocoa
- $1/2$ teaspoon baking powder
- $1/8$ teaspoon salt
-   CHOCOLATE FILLING (recipe follows)
-   Whipped topping or sweetened whipped cream
- 30 HERSHEY'S KISSESBRAND SPECIAL DARK Mildly Sweet Chocolates, unwrapped

1. Heat oven to 350°F. Paper or foil line 30 small ($1^3/4$ inch diameter) muffin cups.

2. Beat butter and shortening in medium bowl until fluffy. Beat in sugar, egg and vanilla. Stir together flour, cocoa, baking powder and salt. Gradually blend into butter mixture, blending well.

3. Drop rounded teaspoonful of dough into prepared muffin cups. Using back of spoon, push dough up sides of muffin cup forming crater in cup. (If you have difficulty with this step, refrigerate pans about 10 minutes and then continue.) Prepare CHOCOLATE FILLING; evenly divide into muffin cups. (Cups will be very full.)

4. Bake 15 minutes or until set. Cool completely in pan on wire rack. Cover; refrigerate until ready to serve. Serve topped with whipped topping and chocolate piece.

Chocolate Filling: Beat 2 packages (3 ounces each) softened cream cheese and $1/4$ cup sugar until well blended. Beat in 1 egg, 1 teaspoon vanilla and $1/8$ teaspoon salt. Place 12 unwrapped HERSHEY'S KISSESBRAND SPECIAL DARK Mildly Sweet Chocolates in small microwave-safe bowl. Microwave at MEDIUM (50%) 15 seconds at a time, stirring after each heating, until chocolates are melted and smooth when stirred. Cool slightly, blend into cheesecake batter.

HUGS & KISSES Crescents

Makes 8 crescents

1   **package (8 ounces) refrigerated crescent dinner rolls**

24 **HERSHEY'S KISSES**BRAND **Milk Chocolates or HERSHEY'S HUGS**BRAND **Candies**

      Powdered sugar

1. Heat oven to 375°F. Separate dough into 8 triangles. Remove wrappers from chocolates.

2. Place 2 chocolates at center of wide end of each triangle; place an additional chocolate on top of other two pieces. Starting at wide end, roll to opposite point; pinch edges to seal. Place rolls, pointed side down, on ungreased cookie sheet. Curve into crescent shape.

3. Bake 10 minutes or until lightly browned. Cool slightly; sift with powdered sugar. Serve warm.

Note

Leftover crescents can be reheated in microwave for a few seconds.

Chocolate Cup Brownie Sundae

Makes 6 cups

CHOCOLATE SHELLS (recipe follows)
Brownie pieces
Ice cream (any flavor)
HERSHEY'S Syrup
Strawberries, blueberries or other fresh fruit slices
Whipped topping or sweetened whipped cream

1. At least 2 hours in advance, prepare CHOCOLATE SHELLS.

2. For each sundae, remove foil from outside of chocolate shell. Place brownie pieces in bottom of chocolate shell. Top with ice cream. Garnish with syrup, fresh fruit and whipped topping.

Chocolate Shells:

1. Line 6 muffin cups (2½ inches in diameter) with foil or paper baking cups. Place 24 unwrapped HERSHEY'S KISSESBRAND Milk Chocolates or HERSHEY'S KISSESBRAND SPECIAL DARK Mildly Sweet Chocolates in medium microwave-safe bowl. Microwave at MEDIUM (50%) 1 minute; stir. If necessary, microwave at MEDIUM an additional 15 seconds at a time, stirring after each heating, until chocolates are melted and smooth when stirred. Cool slightly.

2. Coat inside of pleated surfaces and bottom of bake cups thickly and evenly with melted chocolate using a soft-bristled pastry brush. Refrigerate coated cups 10 minutes or until set; recoat any thin spots with melted chocolate. (If necessary, reheat chocolate on MEDIUM for a few seconds.) Refrigerate cups until very firm, 2 hours or overnight. Cover; refrigerate until ready to use.

Chocolate Quicky Sticky Bread

Makes 12 servings

- 2 loaves (16 ounces each) frozen bread dough
- 3/4 cup granulated sugar
- 1 tablespoon HERSHEY'S Cocoa
- 1 teaspoon ground cinnamon
- 1/2 cup (1 stick) butter or margarine, melted and divided
- 1/2 cup packed light brown sugar
- 1/4 cup water
- HERSHEY'S MINI KISSES BRAND Milk Chocolates

1. Thaw loaves as directed on package; let rise until doubled.

2. Stir together granulated sugar, cocoa and cinnamon. Stir together 1/4 cup butter, brown sugar and water in small microwave-safe bowl. Microwave at MEDIUM (50%) 30 to 60 seconds or until smooth when stirred. Pour mixture into 12-cup fluted tube pan.

3. Heat oven to 350°F. Pinch off pieces of bread dough; form into balls (1 1/2 inches in diameter) placing 3 chocolate pieces inside each ball. Dip each ball in remaining 1/4 cup butter; roll in cocoa-sugar mixture. Place balls in prepared pan.

4. Bake 45 to 50 minutes or until golden brown. Cool 20 minutes in pan; invert onto serving plate. Cool until lukewarm.

HERSHEY'S HUGS & KISSES
Pound Cake Torte

Makes 8 servings

46	HERSHEY'S KISSESBRAND Milk Chocolates
1/3	cup plus 1/2 cup whipping cream, divided
2	teaspoons butter, softened
1/2	teaspoon vanilla extract
1	(10³/4 ounces) frozen loaf pound cake, partially thawed
10	HERSHEY'S HUGSBRAND Candies

1. Remove wrappers from chocolates. Combine chocolates and 1/3 cup whipping cream in small saucepan. Cook over low heat, stirring frequently, until smooth. Remove from heat. Stir in butter and vanilla until smooth; transfer to medium bowl. Refrigerate until firm enough to spread, about 1 hour.

2. Slice cake horizontally to make 3 layers. Arrange bottom layer on serving plate. Evenly spread 1/3 cup chocolate mixture over layer; top with second layer and spread with 1/3 cup mixture. Place remaining layer on top. Beat remaining 1/2 cup whipping cream until thickened; fold in remaining chocolate mixture. Refrigerate a few minutes if a more firm consistency is desired. Frost top, sides and ends of torte. Refrigerate about 6 hours. Remove wrappers from HERSHEY'S HUGSBRAND Candies. Garnish torte before serving. Cover; refrigerate leftover torte.

KISSES Caramel Cheesecake

Makes 10 to 12 servings

COOKIE CRUMB CRUST (recipe follows)

72 HERSHEY'S KISSESʙʀᴀɴᴅ Milk Chocolates filled with Caramels, divided

2¹/₂ teaspoons milk

3 packages (8 ounces each) cream cheese, softened

³/₄ cup sugar

¹/₂ teaspoon vanilla extract

3 eggs

1 teaspoon water

Whipped topping

1. Prepare COOKIE CRUMB CRUST. Heat oven to 350°F.

2. Remove wrappers from caramel filled chocolates. Place 56 chocolates and milk in microwave-safe bowl. Microwave at MEDIUM (50%) 30 seconds; stir. If necessary, microwave at MEDIUM an additional 15 seconds at a time, stirring after each heating, until chocolates are melted and smooth when stirred. Gently pour and spread on bottom of prepared crust.

3. Beat cream cheese, sugar and vanilla in large bowl until smooth. Add eggs, one at a time, beating well after each addition. Gently spoon over caramel mixture.

4. Bake 45 to 50 minutes or until almost set. Remove from oven to wire rack. With knife, loosen cake from side of pan. Cool completely, remove side of pan.

5. Place 4 caramel filled chocolates and water in small microwave-safe bowl. Microwave at MEDIUM 30 seconds or until chocolates are melted and smooth when stirred. Drizzle over surface of cheesecake. Cover; refrigerate until chilled. Garnish with whipped topping and remaining chocolates. Cover; refrigerate leftovers.

Cookie Crumb Crust: Heat oven to 350°F. Stir together 1¹/₂ cups vanilla wafer cookie crumbs (about 45 cookies, crushed) and 1 tablespoon sugar in medium bowl; blend in ¹/₄ cup (¹/₂ stick) melted butter or margarine. Press mixture onto bottom and ¹/₂ inch up side of 9-inch springform pan. Bake 8 minutes; cool.

Double Chocolate Dark Marbled Cheesecake

Makes 10 to 12 servings

CHOCOLATE CRUMB CRUST (recipe follows)

3	packages (8 ounces each) cream cheese, softened
1¼	cups sugar
⅓	cup HERSHEY'S Cocoa
3	eggs
1½	teaspoons vanilla extract
24	HERSHEY'S KISSES_{BRAND} SPECIAL DARK Mildly Sweet Chocolates, divided
	Whipped topping or sweetened whipped cream

1. Prepare CHOCOLATE CRUMB CRUST. Heat oven to 350°F.

2. Beat cream cheese and sugar in large bowl until smooth. Beat in cocoa. Add eggs; one at a time, beating well after each addition. Stir in vanilla. Place ½ cup batter in separate bowl; pour remaining batter into prepared crust.

3. Remove wrappers from 12 chocolates; place in medium microwave-safe bowl. Microwave at MEDIUM (50%) 1 minute; stir. If necessary, microwave at MEDIUM an additional 15 seconds at a time, stirring after each heating, until chocolates are melted and smooth when stirred. Gradually blend melted chocolate into reserved batter. Drop by teaspoons onto batter in pan; swirl with knife or spatula for marbled effect.

4. Bake 45 to 50 minutes or until almost set. Remove from oven to wire rack. With knife, loosen cheesecake from side of pan. Cool completely; remove side of pan. Cover; refrigerate several hours. Garnish with whipped topping and remaining chocolates. Cover; refrigerate leftovers.

Chocolate Crumb Crust: Heat oven to 350°F. Stir together 1¹/₂ cups vanilla wafer crumbs (about 45 cookies, crushed), ¹/₂ cup powdered sugar and ¹/₄ cup HERSHEY'S Cocoa in medium bowl; blend in ¹/₄ cup (¹/₂ stick) melted butter or margarine, mixing well. Press mixture onto bottom and ¹/₂ inch up side of 9-inch springform pan. Bake 8 to 10 minutes; cool.

Easy KISSES Chocolate Tarts

Makes 6 servings

- **48   HERSHEY'S KISSES**BRAND **Milk Chocolates with Almonds, divided**
- **1   cup (¹/₂ pint) whipping cream**
- **6   single serve graham crusts (4-ounce package)**
- **2   to 3 tablespoons chopped toasted almonds***

*To toast almonds: Heat oven to 350°F. Place almonds in thin layer in shallow baking pan. Bake 5 minutes or until almonds are light golden brown, stirring occasionally. Cool completely.

1. Remove wrappers from chocolate pieces. Place 42 chocolates in medium microwave-safe bowl. Microwave at MEDIUM (50%) 1 minute; stir. Microwave at MEDIUM 15 seconds at a time, stirring after each heating, until chocolates are melted when stirred. Cool to room temperature.

2. Beat whipping cream in small bowl until stiff; stir into cooled chocolate, stirring until well blended. Fill crusts. Refrigerate about 2 to 3 hours. Garnish with chopped almonds and remaining chocolate pieces.

Tuxedo Torte

Makes 10 to 12 servings

$1/2$ cup (1 stick) butter or margarine, melted

$1^1/4$ cups granulated sugar

1 teaspoon vanilla extract

2 eggs

$2/3$ cup all-purpose flour

$1/2$ cup HERSHEY'S Cocoa

$1/4$ teaspoon baking powder

$1/4$ teaspoon salt

1 package (8 ounces) cream cheese, softened

1 cup powdered sugar

$3/4$ cup heavy cream, divided

28 HERSHEY'S KISSESBRAND Milk Chocolates*

Whipped topping or sweetened whipped cream (optional)

Additional HERSHEY'S KISSESBRAND Milk Chocolates (optional)

HERSHEY'S HUGSBRAND Candies (optional)

$3/4$ cup HERSHEY'S MINI KISSESBRAND Milk Chocolates may be substituted for HERSHEY'S KISSESBRAND Milk Chocolates.

1. Heat oven to 350°F. Line 9-inch round cake pan with foil, extending foil beyond sides. Grease foil.

2. Stir together melted butter, granulated sugar and vanilla in large bowl. Add eggs; beat well using spoon. Stir together flour, cocoa, baking powder and salt; gradually add to egg mixture, beating with spoon until well blended. Spread batter in prepared pan.

3. Bake 25 minutes or until cake is set. (Cake is fudgey and will not test done.)

Remove from oven; cool completely in pan on wire rack.

4. Beat cream cheese and powdered sugar in medium bowl until well blended. Beat $1/2$ cup heavy cream until stiff; gradually fold into cream cheese mixture, blending well. Spread over brownie layer. Cover; refrigerate at least 1 hour.

5. Remove wrappers from 28 milk chocolates; place in medium microwave-safe bowl with remaining $1/4$ cup heavy cream. Microwave at MEDIUM (50%) 1 minute; stir. If

necessary, microwave at MEDIUM an additional 10 seconds at a time, stirring after each heating, until chocolates are melted and mixture is smooth when stirred. Cool slightly; pour and spread over cream cheese mixture.

6. Cover; refrigerate about 2 hours or until chilled. Use foil to lift out of pan; remove foil. Cut into wedges; serve garnished with whipped topping, chocolates and chocolate candies, if desired. Cover; refrigerate leftover dessert.

HERSHEY'S HUGS and KISSES Candies Chocolate Cake

Makes 12 to 15 servings

³/₄ cup (1¹/₂ sticks) butter or margarine, softened

1³/₄ cups sugar

2 eggs

1 teaspoon vanilla extract

2 cups all-purpose flour

³/₄ cup HERSHEY'S Cocoa or HERSHEY'S SPECIAL DARK Cocoa

1¹/₄ teaspoons baking soda

¹/₂ teaspoon salt

1¹/₃ cups water

COCOA FUDGE FROSTING (recipe follows)

HERSHEY'S HUGSʙʀᴀɴᴅ Candies or HERSHEY'S KISSESʙʀᴀɴᴅ Milk Chocolates

1. Heat oven to 350°F. Grease and flour 13×9×2-inch baking pan.

2. Beat butter and sugar in large bowl until fluffy. Add eggs and vanilla; beat 1 minute on medium speed of mixer. Stir together flour, cocoa, baking soda and salt; add alternately with water to butter mixture, beating until well blended. Pour batter into prepared pan.

3. Bake 40 to 45 minutes or until wooden pick inserted in center comes out clean. Cool 10 minutes; remove from pan to wire rack. Cool completely. Frost with COCOA FUDGE FROSTING. Remove wrappers from candies; garnish cake as desired with candies.

Cocoa Fudge Frosting

Makes about 2¹/₂ cups

¹/₂ cup (1 stick) butter or margarine

¹/₂ cup HERSHEY'S Cocoa or HERSHEY'S SPECIAL DARK Cocoa

3²/₃ cups (1 pound) powdered sugar

¹/₃ cup milk, heated

1 teaspoon vanilla extract

Melt butter in small saucepan over low heat; stir in cocoa. Cook, stirring constantly, until mixture thickens slightly. Remove from heat; pour into small mixer bowl. Add powdered sugar alternately with warm milk, beating to spreading consistency. Stir in vanilla. Spread frosting while warm.

Two Great Tastes Pudding Parfaits

Makes 4 to 6 servings

1 package (6-serving size, 4.6 ounces) vanilla cook and serve pudding and pie filling mix*

3½ cups milk

1 cup REESE'S Peanut Butter Chips

1 cup HERSHEY'S MINI KISSESBRAND Milk Chocolates

Whipped topping (optional)

Additional HERSHEY'S MINI KISSESBRAND Milk Chocolates or grated chocolate

Do not use instant pudding mix.

1. Combine pudding mix and 3½ cups milk in large heavy saucepan (rather than amount listed in package directions). Cook over medium heat, stirring constantly, until mixture comes to a full boil. Remove from heat; divide hot mixture between 2 heatproof medium bowls.

2. Immediately stir peanut butter chips into mixture in one bowl and chocolates into second bowl. Stir both mixtures until chips are melted and mixture is smooth. Cool slightly, stirring occasionally.

3. Alternately layer peanut butter and chocolate mixtures in parfait dishes, wine glasses or dessert dishes. Place plastic wrap directly onto surface of each dessert; refrigerate about 6 hours. Garnish with whipped topping, if desired, and chocolate pieces.

Fun Fact

To celebrate the 100th anniversary of HERSHEY'S KISSES, a giant chocolate was made weighing in at 30,540 pounds.

MINI KISSES
Pumpkin Mousse Cups

Makes 10 servings

1³/₄ cups (10-ounce package) HERSHEY'S MINI KISSESBRAND Milk Chocolates, divided

24 large marshmallows

¹/₂ cup milk

¹/₂ cup canned pumpkin

1 teaspoon vanilla extract

1 teaspoon pumpkin pie spice

¹/₃ cup powdered sugar

1 cup (¹/₂ pint) cold whipping cream

Additional sweetened whipped cream (optional)

1. Line 10 muffin cups (2¹/₂ inches in diameter) with paper bake cups. Reserve ¹/₂ cup chocolate pieces. Place remaining 1¹/₄ cups chocolates in small microwave-safe bowl; microwave at MEDIUM (50%) 1 minute or until melted when stirred. Mixture should be thick.

2. Very thickly coat inside pleated surfaces and bottoms of bake cups with melted chocolate using soft pastry brush. Refrigerate 10 minutes; recoat any thin spots with melted chocolate.* Refrigerate until firm, about 2 hours. Gently peel off paper; refrigerate until ready to fill.

3. Place marshmallows, milk, and pumpkin in medium microwave-safe bowl.

Microwave at MEDIUM 1 minute; stir. Microwave additional 30 seconds at a time, stirring after each heating, until mixture is melted and smooth. Stir in vanilla and pumpkin pie spice. Cool completely.

4. Beat powdered sugar and whipping cream until stiff; fold into pumpkin mixture. Fill cups with pumpkin mousse; garnish with reserved chocolate pieces and sweetened whipped cream, if desired. Cover; refrigerate 2 hours or until firm.

If reheating is needed, microwave chocolate at MEDIUM 15 seconds; stir.

No-Bake Chocolate Cake Roll

Makes about 12 servings

1　package (4-serving size) vanilla instant pudding and pie filling mix

3　tablespoons HERSHEY'S Cocoa, divided

1　cup milk

1　tub (8 ounces) frozen non-dairy whipped topping, thawed and divided

1　package (9 ounces) crisp chocolate wafers

　　HERSHEY'S HUGSʙʀᴀɴᴅ Candies and HERSHEY'S KISSESʙʀᴀɴᴅ Milk Chocolates

1. Combine pudding mix and 2 tablespoons cocoa in small bowl. Add milk; beat on low speed of mixer until smooth and thickened. Fold in 1 cup whipped topping, blending well.

2. Spread about 1 tablespoon pudding mixture onto top of each chocolate wafer; put wafers together in stacks of 4 or 5. On foil, stand wafers on edge to make one long roll. Wrap tightly; refrigerate 5 to 6 hours.

3. Sift remaining 1 tablespoon cocoa over remaining 2½ cups whipped topping; blend well. Unwrap roll; place on serving tray. Spread whipped topping mixture over entire roll. Remove wrappers from candies; place on roll to garnish. To serve, slice diagonally at 45° angle. Cover; refrigerate leftover dessert.

Fun Fact

HERSHEY'S HUGS Chocolates got their name because they look like little KISSES Chocolates being hugged by white chocolate.

Party and Holiday Fun

KISSES Christmas Candies

Makes about 14 candies

About 14 HERSHEY'S KISSES BRAND Milk Chocolates

3/4 cup ground almonds

1/3 cup powdered sugar

1 tablespoon light corn syrup

1/2 teaspoon almond extract

Few drops green food color

Few drops red food color

Granulated sugar

1. Remove wrappers from chocolates. Stir together ground almonds and powdered sugar in medium bowl until well blended. Stir together corn syrup and almond extract; pour over almond mixture, stirring until completely blended. Divide mixture in half, placing each half in separate bowls.

2. Add green food color to one part; with hands, mix until color is well blended and mixture clings together. Add red food color to other half; mix as directed.

3. Shape at least 1 teaspoon colored almond mixture around each chocolate. Roll in granulated sugar. Store in airtight container in cool, dry place.

Sweetheart Layer Bars

Makes about 36 bars

 1   cup (2 sticks) butter or margarine, divided

1¹/₂   cups finely crushed unsalted thin pretzels or pretzel sticks

 1   cup HERSHEY'S MINI KISSES_{BRAND} Milk Chocolates

 1   can (14 ounces) sweetened condensed milk (not evaporated milk)

³/₄   cup HERSHEY'S Cocoa

 2   cups MOUNDS Sweetened Coconut Flakes, tinted*

To tint coconut: Place 1 teaspoon water and ¹/₂ teaspoon red food color in small bowl; stir in 2 cups coconut flakes. With fork, toss until evenly coated.

1. Heat oven to 350°F.

2. Place ³/₄ cup (1¹/₂ sticks) butter in 13×9×2-inch baking pan; place in oven just until butter melts. Remove from oven. Stir in crushed pretzels; press evenly onto bottom of pan. Sprinkle chocolates over pretzel layer.

3. Place sweetened condensed milk, cocoa and remaining ¹/₄ cup (¹/₂ stick) butter in small microwave-safe bowl. Microwave at MEDIUM (50%) 1 to 1¹/₂ minutes or until mixture is melted and smooth when stirred; carefully pour over chocolate layer in pan. Top with coconut; press firmly down onto chocolate layer.

4. Bake 25 to 30 minutes or until lightly browned around edges. Cool completely in pan on wire rack. Cut into heart-shaped pieces with cookie cutters or cut into bars.

KISSES Candy Holiday Twists

Make as desired

1 **bag small pretzels (twisted)**

HERSHEY'S KISSESBRAND **Milk Chocolates**

HERSHEY'S HERSHEY-ETS Candy Coated Milk Chocolates in red and green colors

Additional decorative garnishes such as: small holiday themed candies, nut pieces, miniature marshmallows, candied cherry pieces

1. Heat oven to 350°F. Remove wrappers from chocolates.

2. Place pretzels on ungreased cookie sheet. Place 1 unwrapped chocolate on top of each pretzel.

3. Bake 2 to 3 minutes or until the chocolate starts to soften, but is not melting. (Do not overheat. Melted chocolate retains its shape until disturbed. Heat only until you can gently push chocolate tip down.)

4. Remove from oven; gently press small chocolates and other decorative garnishes on top of the soft chocolate piece. Cool and serve.

HERSHEY'S KISSES Birthday Cake

Makes 10 to 12 servings

2	cups sugar
1³/₄	cups all-purpose flour
³/₄	cup HERSHEY'S Cocoa or HERSHEY'S SPECIAL DARK Cocoa
1¹/₂	teaspoons baking powder
1¹/₂	teaspoons baking soda
1	teaspoon salt
2	eggs
1	cup milk
¹/₂	cup vegetable oil
2	teaspoons vanilla extract
1	cup boiling water
	VANILLA BUTTERCREAM FROSTING (recipe follows)
	HERSHEY'S KISSES₈ʀₐₙᴅ Milk Chocolates

1. Heat oven to 350°F. Grease and flour two (9-inch) round baking pans or one (13×9×2-inch) baking pan.

2. Stir together sugar, flour, cocoa, baking powder, baking soda and salt in large bowl. Add eggs, milk, oil and vanilla; beat with electric mixer on medium speed for 2 minutes. Stir in boiling water (batter will be thin). Pour batter into prepared pans.

3. Bake 30 to 35 minutes for round pans, 35 to 40 minutes for rectangular pan or until wooden pick inserted in center comes out clean. Cool 10 minutes; turn out onto wire racks. Cool completely.

4. Frost with VANILLA BUTTERCREAM FROSTING. Remove wrappers from chocolates. Garnish top and sides of cake with chocolates.

Vanilla Buttercream Frosting

Makes about 2¹/₃ cups

¹/₃	cup butter or margarine, softened
4	cups powdered sugar, divided
3	to 4 tablespoons milk
1¹/₂	teaspoons vanilla extract

Beat butter with electric mixer on medium speed in large bowl until creamy. With mixer running, gradually add about 2 cups powdered sugar, beating until well blended. Slowly beat in milk and vanilla. Gradually add remaining powdered sugar, beating until smooth. Add additional milk, if necessary, until frosting is desired consistency.

Holiday Red Raspberry Chocolate Bars

Makes 36 bars

2¹/₂	cups all-purpose flour
1	cup sugar
³/₄	cup finely chopped pecans
1	egg, beaten
1	cup (2 sticks) cold butter or margarine
1	jar (12 ounces) seedless red raspberry jam
1²/₃	cups HERSHEY'S Milk Chocolate Chips, HERSHEY'S SPECIAL DARK Chocolate Chips, HERSHEY'S Semi-Sweet Chocolate Chips or HERSHEY'S MINI KISSESBRAND Milk Chocolates

1. Heat oven to 350°F. Grease 13×9×2-inch baking pan.

2. Stir together flour, sugar, pecans and egg in large bowl. Cut in butter with pastry blender or fork until mixture resembles coarse crumbs; set aside 1¹/₂ cups crumb mixture. Press remaining crumb mixture on bottom of prepared pan.

Stir jam to soften; carefully spread over crumb mixture in pan. Sprinkle with chocolate chips. Crumble reserved crumb mixture evenly over top.

3. Bake 40 to 45 minutes or until lightly browned. Cool completely in pan on wire rack; cut into bars.

Mini-KISSed Shamrock Cookies

Makes about 2½ dozen cookies

1 pouch (1 pound 1.5 ounces) sugar cookie mix
²/₃ cup HERSHEY'S Cocoa
¹/₃ cup vegetable oil
2 eggs, slightly beaten
1 tablespoon plus 1 teaspoon water
SHAMROCK FROSTING (recipe follows)
HERSHEY'S MINI KISSES BRAND Milk Chocolates

1. Heat oven to 350°F. Combine cookie mix and cocoa in large bowl; stir. Add oil, eggs and water; mix with spoon or fork until well combined. Dough will clump together and be easy to handle.

2. Shape dough into balls, using about 1 level measuring teaspoon dough for each ball. Cluster 3 balls on ungreased cookie sheet to form shamrock; flatten each "leaf" slightly. Shape 1 ball into pencil shape for stem; tuck stem under bottom of shamrock "leaves."

3. Bake 7 to 8 minutes or until set. Cool slightly; remove from cookie sheet to wire rack. Cool completely.

4. Outline shamrock and stem with SHAMROCK FROSTING. Place small amount of frosting in center of each cookie. Press chocolate piece in center.

Shamrock Frosting

1 tablespoon butter or margarine, softened
1 cup powdered sugar
1 tablespoon hot milk or light cream
¹/₂ teaspoon vanilla extract
2 or 3 drops green food color

Mix all ingredients until smooth.

Shower Them with KISSES Cake

Makes 24 servings

- 2 packages (18¼ ounces each) white cake mix, divided
- 2½ cups water, divided
- ⅔ cup vegetable oil, divided
- 4 eggs
- ½ cup sugar, divided
- ¼ cup HERSHEY'S Cocoa, divided
  PREMIER WHITE BUTTERCREAM FROSTING (recipe follows)
  CHOCOLATE BUTTERCREAM FROSTING (recipe follows)
- 2 packages (10 ounces each) HERSHEY'S MINI KISSESBRAND Milk Chocolates
  MILK CHOCOLATE FILIGREE HEARTS (recipe follows)

1. Heat oven to 350°F. Grease and flour 8-inch square baking pan and 8-inch round baking pan. Line bottoms with wax paper; grease and flour paper.

2. Place contents of 1 package cake mix, 1¼ cups water, ⅓ cup vegetable oil and 2 eggs in large bowl; beat until blended. Place 1 cup batter in small bowl; stir in ¼ cup sugar and 2 tablespoons cocoa until blended. Divide vanilla batter evenly into prepared pans; spoon cocoa batter in dollops over top of batter in pans. With knife or spatula, marble chocolate through vanilla batter.

3. Bake 30 to 35 minutes or until wooden pick inserted in center comes out clean. Cool 15 minutes; remove cakes from pans. Remove wax paper; cool completely.

4. Repeat steps 1, 2 and 3.

5. Prepare PREMIER WHITE BUTTERCREAM FROSTING and CHOCOLATE BUTTERCREAM FROSTING. To assemble cake, cover 18×14-inch heavy cardboard with foil. Cut both round layers in half vertically. Arrange 1 square and 2 semi-circles into heart shape. Spread with small amount of frosting; place other square and 2 semi-circles on top. Frost top with white frosting; frost sides with chocolate frosting. Outline entire top and bottom edges of heart-shaped cake with chocolate pieces. Garnish with MILK CHOCOLATE FILIGREE HEARTS, if desired.

Premier White Buttercream Frosting

Makes about 4 cups

2 cups (12-ounce package) HERSHEY'S Premier White Chips

1/3 cup milk

1 1/2 cups (3 sticks) cold butter, cut into pieces

1 3/4 cups powdered sugar

1. Place white chips and milk in large microwave-safe bowl. Microwave at MEDIUM (50%) 1 minute; stir. If necessary, microwave an additional 15 seconds at a time, until mixture is melted and smooth when stirred; cool to lukewarm.

2. Beat butter and powdered sugar gradually into white chip mixture; beat until fluffy.

Chocolate Buttercream Frosting: In bowl, place 2 cups of PREMIER WHITE BUTTERCREAM FROSTING; beat in 2 tablespoons HERSHEY'S Cocoa or HERSHEY'S SPECIAL DARK Cocoa.

Milk Chocolate Filigree Hearts

1 cup HERSHEY'S MINI KISSESBRAND Milk Chocolates

1. Draw desired size heart shapes on paper; cover with wax paper. Place both sheets of paper on baking sheet or tray.

2. Place chocolate pieces in microwave-safe bowl. Microwave at MEDIUM (50%) 30 seconds or just until chocolate is melted when stirred.

3. Pour melted chocolate in small, heavy seal-top plastic bag. With scissors, make small diagonal cut in bottom corner of bag. Pipe thick outlines of heart shapes following heart outlines; fill in center of hearts with a crisscross of chocolate to connect the sides. Refrigerate until firm.

4. Carefully peel wax paper away from chocolate hearts. Place on tray; cover and refrigerate until ready to use as garnishes for cake.

Easy Easter KISSES & Peanut Butter Cup Pie

Makes 8 servings

16	REESE'S Peanut Butter Cups Miniatures, unwrapped and chopped
5¼	cups (12 ounces) frozen non-dairy whipped topping, thawed and divided
2	tablespoons REESE'S Creamy Peanut Butter
1	prepared (6-ounce) graham cracker crumb crust
27	HERSHEY'S KISSES BRAND Milk Chocolates, unwrapped
24	REESE'S Peanut Butter Cups Miniatures or HERSHEY'S KISSES BRAND Milk Chocolates, unwrapped
24	HERSHEY'S Candy-Coated Milk Chocolate Eggs

1. Combine chopped peanut butter cups, 2 cups whipped topping and peanut butter in large bowl. Spread onto bottom of crumb crust.

2. Place 27 milk chocolate pieces in small microwave-safe bowl. Microwave at MEDIUM (50%) 1 minute; stir. If necessary, microwave at MEDIUM an additional 15 seconds at a time, stirring after each heating, until chocolate is melted and smooth when stirred. Stir in 2 cups whipped topping; spread on top of peanut butter layer. Cover; refrigerate until firm.

3. Spread remaining 1¼ cups whipped topping on top of pie. Cut into slices and decorate each slice with 3 chocolates and 3 candy eggs. Serve immediately; refrigerate leftovers.

Fun Fact

The iconic HERSHEY'S KISSES BRAND turned 100 on July 7, 2007.

Edible "Masks"

Makes 2 cookies

- 1   **package (18 ounces) refrigerated sugar cookie dough**
- 3/4   **cup all-purpose flour**
- 1   **can (16 ounces) vanilla ready-to-spread frosting**
-      **Assorted food color**
-      **Decorations, such as ROLO Caramels in Milk Chocolate, HERSHEY'S KISSES**BRAND **Milk Chocolates, York Peppermint Patties, KIT KAT Wafer Bars, REESE'S PIECES Candies, TWIZZLERS PULL-N-PEEL Candy**

1. Heat oven to 350°F. Grease cookie sheet.

2. Combine cookie dough and flour until mixture holds together. Roll dough into 1/4-inch-thick rectangle on lightly floured work surface.

3. Draw two (7- to 8-inch-high) Halloween shapes (pumpkin, ghost, witch, etc.) on cardboard; cut out. Cover them with clear plastic wrap. Place over dough; trace around cardboard pattern with knife. Cut completely through dough. Place shapes on prepared cookie sheet. Using a straw, make one (1/4-inch-wide) hole in each side of "mask" where ear would be.

4. Bake 15 to 20 minutes or until lightly browned. Cool slightly; carefully remove from cookie sheet to wire rack. Cool completely.

5. Divide frosting and tint with food color; frost cookies. Using your imagination, decorate cookies with assorted candies. Separate PULL-N-PEEL candy into strands; tie 1 strand into each hole to resemble strings on a mask.

KISSES Candy Cane Swirl Cheesecake

Makes 10 to 12 servings

COOKIE CRUMB CRUST (recipe follows)
- 3 packages (8 ounces each) cream cheese, softened
- 3/4 cup sugar
- 1 1/2 teaspoons vanilla extract
- 3 eggs
- 42 HERSHEY'S KISSES BRAND Candy Cane Mint Candies, divided
- 1 tablespoon milk
- Sweetened whipped cream

1. Heat oven to 350°F. Prepare COOKIE CRUMB CRUST.

2. Beat cream cheese, sugar and vanilla in large bowl until smooth. Add eggs, one at a time, beating well after each addition. Set aside 1/4 cup batter; spread remaining batter in prepared crust.

3. Remove wrappers from candies. Place 30 candies and milk in medium microwave-safe bowl. Microwave at MEDIUM (50%) 1 minute; stir. If necessary, microwave at MEDIUM 15 seconds at a time, stirring after each heating, until candies are melted and mixture is well blended when stirred. Gradually blend reserved cheesecake batter into candy mixture. Drop candy mixture by tablespoonfuls onto vanilla batter. Gently swirl with knife for marbled effect.

4. Bake 45 to 50 minutes or until center is almost set. Remove from oven to wire rack. With knife, loosen cake from side of pan. Cool completely; remove side of pan. Cover; refrigerate until chilled. Garnish with whipped cream and remaining candies. Cover; refrigerate leftovers.

Cookie Crumb Crust:
Heat oven to 350°F. Stir together 1 1/2 cups vanilla wafer cookie crumbs (about 45 cookies, crushed) and 1 tablespoon sugar in medium bowl; blend in 1/4 cup (1/2 stick) melted butter or margarine. Press mixture onto bottom and 1/2 inch up side of 9-inch springform. Bake 8 minutes; cool.

HERSHEY'S HUGS & KISSES
Valentine's Cake

Makes 10 servings

- **41** HERSHEY'S HUGSBRAND Candies, divided
- **56** HERSHEY'S KISSESBRAND Milk Chocolates, divided
- **³/₄** cup (1¹/₂ sticks) butter or margarine, softened
- **²/₃** cup granulated sugar
- **²/₃** cup packed light brown sugar
- **1¹/₂** teaspoons vanilla extract
- **3** eggs
- **2¹/₂** cups all-purpose flour
- **2** teaspoons baking powder
- **¹/₂** teaspoon salt
- **1** cup milk
- **¹/₃** cup HERSHEY'S Semi-Sweet Chocolate Chips or HERSHEY'S SPECIAL DARK Chocolate Chips
- **1** teaspoon shortening
- WHIPPED CREAM FROSTING (recipe follows)

1. Heat oven to 350°F. Grease and line bottoms of two (9-inch) heart-shaped baking pans with wax paper.* Remove wrappers from 24 HUGS Candies and 24 KISSES Chocolates; chop into ¹/₄-inch pieces.

2. Beat butter, granulated sugar, brown sugar and vanilla in large bowl until creamy. Add eggs; beat well. Stir together flour, baking powder and salt. Add flour mixture alternately with milk to butter mixture, beating well after each addition. Stir in chopped chocolate. Pour batter into prepared pans.

3. Bake 25 to 30 minutes or until wooden pick inserted in center comes out clean. Cool 10 minutes in pans on wire racks. Remove from pans; cool completely.

4. Place chocolate chips and shortening in small microwave-safe bowl. Microwave at Medium (50%) 30 seconds to 1 minute or until chocolate is melted when stirred. Trace 5-inch heart shape on paper; place wax paper over top. Place melted chip mixture in bottom of sturdy seal-top plastic bag; using scissors, snip off small corner at bottom. Pipe melted chocolate over heart; refrigerate until firm.

5. Prepare WHIPPED CREAM FROSTING; reserve 1 cup. Frost between layers, sides and top of cake. Place reserved frosting in a clean sturdy seal-top plastic bag with star tip; pipe rosettes along top of cake. Unwrap remaining 17 HUGS Candies; place on top of rosettes. Unwrap remaining 32 KISSES Chocolates; place along bottom edge of cake. Remove chocolate heart from wax paper; place in center of cake. Cover and refrigerate cake.

*Two (9-inch) round baking pans can be used in place of heart-shaped pans, if desired.

Whipped Cream Frosting:
Place 1 tablespoon cold water in small cup; sprinkle 1 teaspoon unflavored gelatin over top. Let stand several minutes to soften. Stir in 2 tablespoons boiling water until gelatin is completely dissolved and mixture is clear. Beat 2 cups (1 pint) cold whipping cream and 1/3 cup powdered sugar in large bowl until stiff. Pour in gelatin mixture; beat until well blended and thickened. Stir in 5 drops red food color, if desired. Makes about 4 cups frosting.

Jack-O-Lantern Brownie

Makes 12 to 16 servings

³/₄ cup (1¹/₂ sticks) butter or margarine, melted

1¹/₂ cups sugar

1¹/₂ teaspoons vanilla extract

3 eggs

³/₄ cup all-purpose flour

¹/₂ cup HERSHEY'S Cocoa

¹/₂ teaspoon baking powder

¹/₄ teaspoon salt

Yellow and red food color

1 can (16 ounces) canned vanilla frosting

Garnishes: HERSHEY'S MINI KISSES BRAND Milk Chocolates, TWIZZLERS NIBS Licorice Bits, TWIZZLERS PULL-N-PEEL, HEATH English Toffee Bits, assorted candies

1. Heat oven to 350°F. Grease 12-inch round pizza pan. If using a disposable pan, place on baking sheet to bake.

2. Beat melted butter, sugar and vanilla with spoon in large bowl. Beat in eggs. Stir in dry ingredients; beat with spoon until well blended. Spread in pan.

3. Bake 20 to 22 minutes or until top springs back when touched lightly in center. Cool completely. Add yellow and red food color to frosting for desired shade of orange. Frost brownie; garnish to resemble a jack-o-lantern.

Tip
To celebrate other holidays, simply change the frosting color and garnishes.

HERSHEY'S Gridiron Cake

Makes about 18 servings

GRIDIRON CAKE (recipe follows)

1 tablespoon HERSHEY'S Cocoa or HERSHEY'S SPECIAL DARK Cocoa

1 can (16 ounces) creamy vanilla ready-to-spread frosting, divided

Green, red and yellow food color

1²/₃ cups HERSHEY'S Premier White Chips

1 package (8 ounces) REESE'S PIECES Candy

11 HERSHEY'S KISSESBRAND Milk Chocolates

11 REESE'S Peanut Butter Cups Miniatures

3 HERSHEY'S HUGSBRAND Candies

6 ROLO Caramels in Milk Chocolate

2 TWIZZLERS Strawberry Twists

1. Prepare GRIDIRON CAKE. For chocolate frosting, stir cocoa into ¹/₃ cup frosting; stir until smooth. Tint ¹/₃ cup frosting orange with 1 drop red food color and 2 drops yellow food color; stir until blended. Tint remaining frosting green with 2 or 3 drops green food color; stir until blended.

2. Mark "end zones", 2 inches wide at each end of cake, using wooden pick; frost one end zone with chocolate frosting and the other end zone with

orange frosting. Frost the area between end zones with green frosting; mark 5 yard lines with wooden pick. Place white chips all across cake on yard lines.

3. Use white chips to spell out "HERSHEY'S" on chocolate end zone; use brown REESE'S PIECES on the goal line. Use yellow REESE'S PIECES to spell out "REESE'S" on orange end zone. Use orange REESE'S PIECES on the goal line.

4. Remove wrappers from chocolates and peanut butter cups. Arrange teams on cake playing field, using HERSHEY'S KISSES Milk Chocolates as one team and peanut butter cups as second team. Place HERSHEY'S HUGS Candies as referee officials on the field.

5. Unwrap ROLOs; for goal posts, stack 3 ROLOs in the middle of each goal line on each side of field. Cut end off twists; insert wooden picks to form "U" shapes for goal posts. "Glue" with frosting to top of each stack of ROLOs.

Gridiron Cake

1	cup water
1	cup (2 sticks) butter or margarine
1/2	cup HERSHEY'S Cocoa
2	cups sugar
1 3/4	cups all-purpose flour
1	teaspoon baking soda
1/2	teaspoon salt
3	eggs
3/4	cup dairy sour cream

1. Heat oven to 350°F. Grease and flour 15 1/2×10 1/2×1-inch disposable foil baking pan or jelly-roll pan.

2. Combine water, butter and cocoa in medium saucepan. Cook over medium heat, stirring occasionally, until mixture boils. Boil 1 minute. Remove from heat; set aside.

3. Stir together sugar, flour, baking soda and salt in large bowl. Add eggs and sour cream; beat until blended. Add cocoa mixture; beat just until blended (batter will be thin). Pour into prepared pan.

4. Bake 25 to 30 minutes or until wooden pick inserted in center comes out clean. Cool cake in pan on wire rack.

Tip

Change frosting color for end zones to match your favorite team colors.

HERSHEY'S Firecracker Cake

Makes 8 to 10 servings

 4 eggs, separated

$^1/_2$ cup plus $^1/_3$ cup granulated sugar, divided

 1 teaspoon vanilla extract

$^1/_2$ cup all-purpose flour

$^1/_3$ cup HERSHEY'S Cocoa

$^1/_4$ teaspoon baking powder

$^1/_4$ teaspoon baking soda

$^1/_8$ teaspoon salt

$^1/_3$ cup water

    Powdered sugar

 1 cup cherry pie filling

 1 tub (8 ounces) frozen whipped topping, thawed and divided

    HERSHEY'S KISSES BRAND Milk Chocolates, HERSHEY'S HUGS BRAND Candies, HERSHEY'S MINIATURES Chocolate Bars

    Blueberries, raspberries, halved strawberries

 1 TWIZZLERS Strawberry Twists

1. Heat oven to 375°F. Line 15$^1/_2$×10$^1/_2$×1-inch jelly-roll pan with foil; generously grease foil.

2. Beat egg whites in large bowl until foamy; gradually add $^1/_2$ cup granulated sugar, beating until stiff peaks form.

3. Beat egg yolks and vanilla in small bowl on high speed of mixer about 3 minutes. Gradually add remaining $^1/_3$ cup granulated sugar; continue beating 2 minutes. Combine flour, cocoa, baking powder, baking soda and salt; add to egg yolk mixture alternately with water on low speed, beating just until batter is smooth.

4. Fold chocolate mixture gradually into egg whites; spread evenly in prepared pan.

5. Bake 12 to 15 minutes or until top springs back when touched lightly in center. Immediately loosen cake from edges of pan; invert on towel sprinkled with powdered sugar. Carefully remove foil. Immediately roll cake in towel, starting from narrow end; place on wire rack to cool.

6. Unroll cake; remove towel. Spread with pie filling and 1½ cups whipped topping; reroll cake. Frost cake with remaining whipped topping. Place candies and fruit on frosted cake so that they form stripes around the cake. Add strawberry twist for "wick." Refrigerate until serving time.

KISSES Candy Cane Blossoms

Makes about 4 dozen cookies

- 48 HERSHEY'S KISSESBRAND Candy Cane Mint Candies
- 1/2 cup (1 stick) butter or margarine, softened
- 1 cup granulated sugar
- 1 egg
- 1 1/2 teaspoons vanilla extract
- 2 cups all-purpose flour
- 1/4 teaspoon baking soda
- 1/4 teaspoon salt
- 2 tablespoons milk
- Red or green sugar crystals, granulated sugar or powdered sugar

1. Heat oven to 350°F. Remove wrappers from candies.

2. Beat butter, granulated sugar, egg and vanilla in large bowl until well blended. Stir together flour, baking soda and salt; add alternately with milk to butter mixture, beating until well blended.

3. Shape dough into 1-inch balls. Roll in red sugar, granulated sugar, powdered sugar or a combination of any of the sugars. Place on ungreased cookie sheet.

4. Bake 8 to 10 minutes or until edges are lightly browned and cookie is set. Remove from oven; cool 2 to 3 minutes. Press a candy piece into center of each cookie. Remove from cookie sheet to wire rack. Cool completely.

Easter Baskets and Bunnies Cupcakes

Makes about 33 cupcakes

2 cups sugar

1³/₄ cups all-purpose flour

³/₄ cup HERSHEY'S Cocoa or HERSHEY'S SPECIAL DARK Cocoa

1¹/₂ teaspoons baking powder

1¹/₂ teaspoons baking soda

1 teaspoon salt

2 eggs

1 cup milk

¹/₂ cup vegetable oil

2 teaspoons vanilla extract

1 cup boiling water

CREAMY VANILLA FROSTING (recipe follows)

Green, red and yellow food color

3³/₄ cups MOUNDS Sweetened Coconut Flakes, divided and tinted*

Suggested garnishes: marshmallows, HERSHEY'S MINI KISSES BRAND Milk Chocolates, licorice, jelly beans

To tint coconut: Combine ³/₄ teaspoon water with several drops green food color in small bowl. Stir in 1¹/₄ cups coconut. Toss with fork until evenly tinted. Repeat with red and yellow food color and remaining coconut.

1. Heat oven to 350°F. Line muffin cups (2¹/₂ inches in diameter) with paper bake cups.

2. Stir together sugar, flour, cocoa, baking powder, baking soda and salt in large bowl. Add eggs, milk, oil and vanilla; beat on medium speed of mixer 2 minutes. Stir in boiling water (batter will be thin). Fill muffin cups ²/₃ full with batter.

3. Bake 22 to 25 minutes or until wooden pick inserted in center comes out clean. Cool completely. Prepare CREAMY VANILLA FROSTING; frost cupcakes. Immediately press desired color tinted coconut onto each cupcake. Garnish as desired.

Creamy Vanilla Frosting: Beat ¹/₃ cup softened butter or margarine in medium bowl. Add 1 cup powdered sugar and 1¹/₂ teaspoons vanilla extract; beat well. Add 2¹/₂ cups powdered sugar alternately with ¹/₄ cup milk, beating to spreading consistency. Makes about 2 cups frosting.

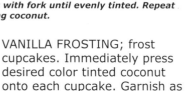

KISSES Crafts

HERSHEY'S Pinwheel Party Favors

MATERIALS:

- Scissors
- Construction paper/double-sided scrapbook paper
- Ruler
- Pencil
- Glue (low-temperature glue gun and glue sticks, non-toxic craft glue, glue stick or safe confectioners' glue)*
- HERSHEY'S KISSESBRAND Chocolates
- 6-inch lengths of 12-gauge floral wire
- Straws

*Use hot melt glue with adult supervision. Safe confectioners' glue recipe on page 106.

INSTRUCTIONS:

1. Cut a 6-inch square out of the construction paper.

2. Place a ruler diagonally, corner to corner and draw a line with the pencil. Repeat with the other 2 corners.

3. Cut each line beginning at the outside corner and ending within an inch of the center of the square.

4. One at a time, fold each corner to the center of the square and glue. When all 4 corners are glued, you have formed the pinwheel.

5. Glue the flat side of 1 chocolate to the center of the pinwheel.

6. Insert 1 end of the floral wire through the back center of the pinwheel into the chocolate.

7. Slip the straw over the remaining length of the floral wire.

8. Holding onto only the straw, blow gently on the pinwheel and watch it spin.

Note: Completed craft is for decorative purpose only. Candy should not be eaten.

Small KISSES Christmas Tree

MATERIALS FOR ONE TREE:

- Ice cream sugar cone
- Aluminum foil
- Glue (low-temperature glue gun and glue sticks, non-toxic craft glue, glue stick or safe confectioners' glue)*
- 26 to 30 HERSHEY'S KISSESBRAND Chocolates in holiday foil
- $^1/_3$ yard ($^1/_4$-inch-wide) ribbon (optional)

*Use hot melt glue with adult supervision. Safe confectioners' glue recipe on page 106.

INSTRUCTIONS:

Cover each cone with aluminum foil, securing with glue. Push remaining foil inside open end of cone to add strength. Glue chocolates onto cone with the flat end of the chocolate on the foil surface. Begin around the base and work up to the top, alternating colors. Finish by adding a small bow to the top, if desired.

Finished Size: 5 inches high.

Note: Completed craft is for decorative purpose only. Candy should not be eaten.

KISSES Crafts

HERSHEY'S HUGS & KISSES
Chocolate Cards

MATERIALS:

- **Store-bought cards**
- **Construction paper, scrapbook papers**
- **Scraps of ribbon, trims, embellishments, etc.**
- **Glue (low-temperature glue gun and glue sticks, non-toxic craft glue, glue stick or safe confectioners' glue)***
- **HERSHEY'S KISSES**BRAND **Milk Chocolates and HERSHEY'S HUGS**BRAND **Candies**

*Use hot melt glue with adult supervision. Safe confectioners' glue recipe on page 106.

INSTRUCTIONS:

Create sweet and original cards to carry your wishes. Decorate a homemade card, a computer-generated card or even a store-bought card with HERSHEY'S HUGSBRAND Candies or KISSESBRAND Chocolates and make your message even more personal. Use some of our ideas in the picture or create your own.

Note: Completed craft is for decorative purpose only. Candy should not be eaten.

HERSHEY'S HUGS & KISSES
Sweetheart Roses

MATERIALS:

- Glue (low-temperature glue gun and glue sticks, non-toxic craft glue, glue stick or safe confectioners' glue)*
- HERSHEY'S KISSESBRAND Chocolates or HUGSBRAND Candies, in pink and red foils
- Florist wire
- Clear cellophane or plastic wrap
- Florist tape
- Artificial leaves (optional)
- Ribbon

Use hot melt glue with adult supervision. Safe confectioners' glue recipe follows.

INSTRUCTIONS:

1. For each candy rose, spread confectioners' glue on bottom of one foil-wrapped chocolate. Firmly press the bottom of another chocolate to it.

2. Insert florist wire into one pointed end of double chocolate. Wrap 4-inch square of clear cellophane around double chocolate, twisting cellophane tightly around chocolate.

3. Starting at bottom of rose, wrap florist tape around edges of cellophane, continuing down the full length of wire with tape. Add 1 or 2 artificial leaves, if desired, securing leaves in place with florist tape.

4. Tie two or more candy roses together with a bow.

Note: Completed craft is for decorative purpose only. Candy should not be eaten.

Safe confectioners' glue:

Gently stir together 4 teaspoons pasteurized dried egg whites (meringue powder) and 1/4 cup warm water until completely dissolved. Beat in 3 cups sifted powdered sugar until thick and smooth. Use immediately. Cover with wet paper towel to keep from drying out.

Tip
You can make these into a bouquet or set in a vase for display.

HERSHEY'S KISSES Snowflake

MATERIALS:

- Pencil
- White poster board (about 3- to 4-inch square)
- Plastic cup or drinking glass
- Decorative-edged scissors designed for children
- 4 paint stirring sticks (available at paint stores)
- Glue (low-temperature glue gun and glue sticks, non-toxic craft glue, glue stick or safe confectioners' glue)*
- Silver metallic acrylic craft paint (or color of choice)
- 1/2-inch paint brush
- 6-inch length of ribbon (1/2-inch wide)
- 1 thumbtack
- 14 HERSHEY'S KISSESBRAND Chocolates wrapped in holiday foil
- 4 silver and white glitter pipe cleaners
- Silver glitter glue

*Use hot melt glue with adult supervision. Safe confectioners' glue recipe on page 106.

INSTRUCTIONS:

1. Trace a 3-inch circle onto the poster board using the bottom of a plastic cup or glass as a template. Cut out the circle using the decorative-edged scissors.

2. Place a generous amount of glue in the center of each paint stick. To make the snowflake shape: first glue two sticks together in the center to form a cross shape. Add the next

two sticks, overlapping them so that the result looks like eight evenly-spaced spokes on a wheel.

3. Paint both sides of the snowflake using the metallic paint. Let dry about 1 hour.

4. Place the poster board circle on top. Let dry for a few hours.

5. Fold the ribbon in half and, with the thumbtack, attach it to the underside of the top of one of the paint sticks to create a loop for hanging.

6. Glue a chocolate on the end of each paint stick and glue six chocolates in the circle (one in the center and five around it), or glue them onto the sticks as desired.

7. Cut each pipe cleaner in half, and bend each to form a V-shape and glue one on each stick, about an inch or two below the chocolates.

Note: Completed craft is for decorative purpose only. Candy should not be eaten.

Star of David Ornament

MATERIALS:

- **6 craft sticks**
- **Glitter**
- **Glue (low-temperature glue gun and glue sticks, non-toxic craft glue, glue stick or safe confectioners' glue)***
- **6 HERSHEY'S KISSES**BRAND **Chocolates filled with Caramel**
- **Embroidery thread**

*Use hot melt glue with adult supervision. Safe confectioners' glue recipe on page 106.

INSTRUCTIONS:

1. Make Star of David shapes from craft sticks. Glue together.

2. Add glitter on each star.

3. Glue a chocolate to each tip of star.

4. Add thread at each end to hang in home.

Note: Completed craft is for decorative purpose only. Candy should not be eaten.

KISSES Crafts

Spring Birdhouse Centerpiece

MATERIALS:

- 1 Styrofoam sheet (1×12×36 inches)
- Pencil
- Scissors
- 1 square of green felt, 2 of blue felt and 1 of yellow felt
- Glue (low-temperature glue gun and glue sticks, non-toxic craft glue, glue stick or safe confectioners' glue)*
- 5 wooden skewers
- Toothpicks
- 4 bags (10 to 11 ounces each) HERSHEY'S KISSESBRAND Chocolates in spring colors
- Floral wire
- Feather butterfly wings
- Spanish moss
- Small bird

Use hot melt glue with adult supervision. Safe confectioners' glue recipe on page 106.

INSTRUCTIONS:

1. From a Styrofoam sheet, cut the four pieces of the birdhouse. Cut one (9×4-inch) piece to form the base, cut two (6×2-inch) pieces for the roof, then cut the front and back of the house using pattern provided (Figure 1).

2. Cover the base with green felt. Cut out two pieces from the blue felt to cover the Styrofoam of the front and back of the house. (Remember to cut out the hole in the center of both pieces.)

3. To assemble, place house in the center of the base, secure in place by using glue and 4 wooden skewers. Secure by inserting each skewer through the top of the house down through the base. (Figure 2.)

4. Attach the roof pieces using glue and securing with toothpicks. Cover both sides with yellow felt.

5. Decorate the birdhouse from the base up by gluing the flat end of the chocolates, spring colors, to the flat surface of the house. (Remember to decorate both sides if you plan to use as a table centerpiece.

6. To make the springy buds in the garden, cut 5-inch lengths of floral wire and twirl each piece around a pencil to form the spring. Insert one end of wire into bottom of a pink

KISSES Chocolate and the other end into the green base.

7. To make the butterfly, glue two chocolates' flat ends together with the feather wings between the chocolates. Using the same instructions as the springy buds, take a coiled wire and insert one end into the chocolate and the other end into the roof.

8. Complete by creating a nest out of Spanish moss for our bird to sit on. Insert a wooden skewer cut to 3-inch length through the house below the bird's nest for a perch.

Finished size:
10 inches high ×9 inches wide.

Note: Completed craft is for decorative purpose only. Candy should not be eaten.

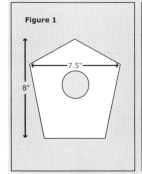

Figure 1

7.5"

8"

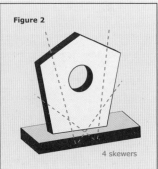

Figure 2

4 skewers

KISSES Crafts

HERSHEY'S KISSES
Wreath Ornament

MATERIALS:

- Plastic or wooden drapery rings (available at most craft & fabric stores)
- Aluminum foil
- Glue (low-temperature glue gun and glue sticks, non-toxic craft glue, glue stick or safe confectioners' glue)*
- 26 to 30 HERSHEY'S KISSES BRAND Chocolates in holiday foil
- 1/3 yard (1/4-inch-wide) ribbon

*Use hot melt glue with adult supervision. Safe confectioners' glue recipe on page 106.

INSTRUCTIONS:

Cover the drapery ring with aluminum foil. Decorate by gluing flat end of chocolates to the foil surface. Complete by tying ribbon bow onto the eye hook on the ring.

Finished Size: 4-inch wreath.

Note: Completed craft is for decorative purpose only. Candy should not be eaten.

KISSES Crafts

HERSHEY'S KISSES Mice

MATERIALS:

- ¹/₄ yard of ¹/₂-inch pink grosgrain ribbon
- Scissors
- Glue (low-temperature glue gun and glue sticks, non-toxic craft glue, glue stick or safe confectioners' glue)*
- 4 HERSHEY'S KISSES_{BRAND} Chocolates per pair of mice
- 1 sheet pink felt
- 4 jiggly eyes

Use hot melt glue with adult supervision. Safe confectioners' glue recipe on page 106.

INSTRUCTIONS:

Note: Completed craft is for decorative purpose only. Candy should not be eaten.

1. Create tails by cutting 2-inch lengths of pink grosgrain ribbons, pinch one end of the ribbon in half and glue to point of one chocolate.

2. Cut the ears out of the pink felt and glue the base of the heart shape to the top of the flat side of one chocolate, leaving the two curved shapes extending over the edge to form the ears.

3. Glue both chocolates together flat end to flat end with felt ears nesting in between.

4. Complete by gluing on the jiggly eyes.

113

HERSHEY'S KISSES
Chocolates Sweet Menorah

MATERIALS:

- 1 (9×1-inch) round Styrofoam disc
- Scissors
- 2 yards (1-inch-wide) blue ribbon
- Glue (low-temperature glue gun and glue sticks, non-toxic craft glue, glue stick or safe confectioners' glue)*
- 2 (10-inch) silver foil doilies
- 1 (4×2-inch) round Styrofoam disc
- Aluminum foil
- 10 bamboo skewers
- 3 bags (10 to 11 ounces each) HERSHEY'S KISSESBRAND Milk Chocolates, wrapped in silver foil
- 9 (1-inch-diameter) silver foil candy cups
- 3 sheets blue construction paper
- 18 HERSHEY'S KISSESBRAND Milk Chocolates, wrapped in red foil

Use hot melt glue with adult supervision. Safe confectioners' glue recipe on page 106.

INSTRUCTIONS:

1. To create base of menorah, cut 9×1-inch Styrofoam disk in half. Glue blue ribbon along the curved outsized edges of each half disk. Cover the flat side of each half disk by folding one silver doily over each half, lining up the curved edges; secure with glue.

2. Cover 4×2-inch disk with foil; glue blue ribbon around outside edge.

3. To assemble menorah, place one half disk flat on surface, curved side facing forward. Put 4×2-inch disk, flat side down, in center of half disk. Secure with glue. Place other half disk, curved side down, in center of 4×2-inch disk. Secure with 3 skewers and glue, piercing through all three pieces. (See illustration.) Decorate by gluing chocolates to base.

4. Add candle holders by gluing 9 silver candy cups along the top edge of base.

5. To make candles, cut blue construction paper into 8 (4× 4-inch each) pieces and 1 piece 5×4-inch for the center candle. Roll each piece into a 3/4-inch diameter cylinder; secure with glue. Cut 5 skewers in half; glue each skewer to inside of candle; insert the excess length of each skewer into each candy cup.

Finished Size:
13 inches high×10 inches wide.

Note: Completed craft is for decorative purpose only. Candy should not be eaten.

HERSHEY'S KISSES
Picture Frame Ornament

MATERIALS:

- Poster board, craft foam or cardstock in two different colors, cut into 3 (7-inch) squares (2 in one color, 1 in the other color)
- Pencil
- Straight-edged scissors
- Decorative-edged scissors
- Plastic cup or drinking glass
- Glue stick for poster board/cardstock or non-toxic craft glue for craft foam
- Photo or color copy to frame
- 15 HERSHEY'S KISSESBRAND Chocolates filled with Caramel
- 12-inch decorative ribbon and yarn or wire ribbon

Use hot melt glue with adult supervision.

INSTRUCTIONS:

1. Trace a smaller star shape* onto one piece of the poster board. Cut out the stars using the straight-edged scissors.

2. Use a larger star shape to trace and cut out another star with the decorative-edged or regular scissors.

3. Trace a circle on one of the small stars using a plastic cup or drinking glass as a template. Cut out the circle.

4. With glue stick (for poster board) or craft glue (for craft foam) glue the photo behind the small star with the circle. Glue the two pieces together, with the largest star on the back, the small, solid star in back, and the small star with the photo on top. Let dry 1 hour.

5. Decorate with chocolates and let dry.

6. Punch out a small, ⅛-inch hole at top of shape. Insert yarn or wire ribbon through hole and tie. Hang on holiday tree.

You can also make these in a circle or other shape, if desired.

Note: Completed craft is for decorative purpose only. Candy should not be eaten.

HUGS & KISSES Candy Box

MATERIALS:

- **72** to 74 HERSHEY'S KISSES BRAND Milk Chocolates, divided
- **2** tablespoons shortening (do not use butter, margarine, spread or oil)
- **10** HERSHEY'S HUGS BRAND Candies, unwrapped
- **11** HERSHEY'S MINIATURES Chocolate Bars, unwrapped

HERSHEY'S POT OF GOLD Truffles/HERSHEY'S BLISS Milk Chocolates

INSTRUCTIONS:

1. Trace two (6½-inch) heart shapes on paper; place on baking sheet. Top with wax paper.

2. Remove wrappers from KISSES Milk Chocolates, reserving 10 chocolates for decoration. Place remaining chocolate pieces and shortening in medium microwave-safe bowl. Microwave at MEDIUM (50%) 1 minute; stir. If necessary, microwave at MEDIUM an additional 15 seconds at a time, stirring after each heating, until chocolate is melted and smooth when stirred.

3. Set aside ¼ cup melted chocolate. Spread half of remaining chocolate on wax paper over each heart shape. Refrigerate until firm.

4. For candy box top, dip bottom of reserved KISSES Chocolates and HUGS Candies in remaining melted chocolate and alternately press in place along edge of heart. For candy box bottom, dip long edge and sides of small chocolate bars in melted chocolate. Press along edge of heart. Cut one chocolate bar in half for top of heart. Refrigerate until firm.

5. Fill candy box with truffles or chocolates. Store in cool place or refrigerate.

KISSES Crafts

Spring Topiary Centerpiece

MATERIALS:

- Styrofoam topiary form (available at most craft stores)
- Clay or plastic flower pot
- Aluminum foil
- 3 bags (10 to 11 ounces each) HERSHEY'S KISSESBRAND Chocolates in spring colors
- Glue (low-temperature glue gun and glue sticks, non-toxic craft glue, glue stick or safe confectioners' glue)*
- Toothpicks
- Spanish moss
- 2 yards of 1-inch-wide ribbon

*Use hot melt glue with adult supervision. Safe confectioners' glue recipe on page 106.

INSTRUCTIONS:

1. Place the Styrofoam topiary base into a clay or plastic flower pot.

2. Cover both ball shapes with aluminum foil. Cover each ball shape with spring colored chocolates by gluing the flat end of the chocolate to topiary. With remaining chocolates, fill in gaps by inserting a toothpick in the side of a chocolate and inserting the other end into the foam ball. Alternate colors and angles.

3. Complete by covering top of foam base with Spanish moss and tie a ribbon bow around both sections of the stem. Sprinkle extra chocolates on the table surface like falling petals, and let your guests sample your artwork.

Finished Size: 16-inches tall.

Note: Completed craft is for decorative purpose only. Candy should not be eaten.

Tip

Change up the color of your centerpiece for holidays all year long.

HERSHEY'S KISSES Kritters

- Glue (low-temperature glue gun and glue sticks, non-toxic craft glue, glue stick or safe confectioners' glue)*
- Butterfly wings/feathers (available at craft stores or make your own)
- 2 HERSHEY'S KISSESBRAND Chocolates per Kritter
- Pipe cleaner
- Construction paper, felt or foam sheets
- Jiggly eyes

*Use hot melt glue with adult supervision. Safe confectioners' glue recipe on page 106.

INSTRUCTIONS:

Butterfly KISS

1. Glue 1 pair of butterfly wings to the flat side of one chocolate.

2. Bend a 2-inch piece of pipe cleaner in half and curl both ends.

3. Glue folded point to top end of same chocolate.

4. Glue second chocolate flat end to flat end with other chocolate, securing the wings and antennae between them.

5. Complete by gluing on jiggly eyes.

KISS Katerpillar

1. Curl a 6-inch piece of pipe cleaner around a pencil. Glue one chocolate to each end of the curled pipe cleaner.

2. Fold a 1-inch piece of pipe cleaner in half and glue to top of one chocolate to form antennae.

3. Cut two sets of feet. Glue to bottom of each chocolate.

4. Complete by gluing on jiggly eyes.

KISS Ostrich

1. Bend pipe cleaner in half.

2. Glue the center of the bent pipe cleaner to an edge of the flat side of a chocolate.

3. Glue feather to the opposite edge of the flat side of the same chocolate.

4. Glue second chocolate flat end to flat end with other chocolate, securing the feather and pipe cleaner in between them.

5. Complete by gluing on jiggly eyes to one chocolate and feathers to the sides of the other chocolate.

Note: Completed craft is for decorative purpose only. Candy should not be eaten.

HERSHEY'S KISSeltoe Ball

MATERIALS:

- **Wire coat hanger**
- **4-, 6- or 8-inch Styrofoam ball**
- **Aluminum foil (optional)**
- **Glue (low-temperature glue gun and glue sticks, non-toxic craft glue, glue stick or safe confectioners' glue)***
- **4 to 8 bags (10 to 11 ounces each) HERSHEY'S KISSES**BRAND **Chocolates, wrapped in green, red and silver foil (ball size will determine how many bags are needed)**
- **Toothpicks**
- **4 yards (1-inch-wide) holiday ribbon**

**Use hot melt glue with adult supervision. Safe confectioners' glue recipe on page 106.*

INSTRUCTIONS:

1. Straighten the wire hanger; insert one end through the center of the Styrofoam ball. Clear 6 inches of wire through opposite end; bend a hook at least 1 inch in length. Pull wire back up through hole, securing hooked end into bottom of foam ball. Determine desired length of top wire. Bend loop at end to form hanger. (Hang on ladder or clothes rod to decorate.)

2. Cover ball with aluminum foil, if desired. Cover ball by gluing green foil-wrapped chocolates with the flat end to the surface of the ball. Decorate with remaining silver and red chocolates by inserting end of toothpick into the side of a chocolate; insert other end into ball, filling in any gaps. Alternate colors and angles.

3. Finish by attaching a large bow on top and loops of ribbon on the bottom.

Note: Completed craft is for decorative purpose only. Candy should not be eaten.

KISSES Crafts

Angelic HUGS Candies Centerpiece

MATERIALS:

- 1 (12×4-inch) foam cone
- Aluminum foil
- 1 (4-inch) foam ball
- Toothpicks
- Glue (low-temperature glue gun and glue sticks, non-toxic craft glue, glue stick or safe confectioners' glue)*
- 3 (12-inch) white paper doilies
- 2 T pins
- 4 to 5 bags (10 to 11 ounces each) HERSHEY'S HUGSBRAND Candies
- Cardboard
- Scissors
- Yellow curling ribbon
- Light blue ribbon
- Blue and red felt

Use hot melt glue with adult supervision. Safe confectioners' glue recipe on page 106.

INSTRUCTIONS:

1. Cut 2 inches off the tip of the foam cone to create a flat base for the angel's head to rest. Cover cone with foil. Attach 4-inch foam ball; secure with toothpicks and glue.

2. To create wings, make a single cut in each of 2 doilies from the outside edge to the center; create a fan with accordion folds. Attach fan to each side of the angel using a T pin. Decorate cone with HUGS Candies by gluing their flat sides against the foil-covered cone.

3. Cut a moon shape out of the cardboard for the halo that will rest on the angel's head. Cover with paper doilies; glue HUGS Candies to halo. Set on the angel's head. Cover the back of the head with chocolates. Finish by adding curled pieces of ribbon for hair; tie ribbon around her neck and attach felt eyes and mouth with a dab of glue.

Note: Completed craft is for decorative purpose only. Candy should not be eaten.

Index

Index

Index

Index

METRIC CONVERSION CHART

VOLUME MEASUREMENTS (dry)

1/8 teaspoon = 0.5 mL
1/4 teaspoon = 1 mL
1/2 teaspoon = 2 mL
3/4 teaspoon = 4 mL
1 teaspoon = 5 mL
1 tablespoon = 15 mL
2 tablespoons = 30 mL
1/4 cup = 60 mL
1/3 cup = 75 mL
1/2 cup = 125 mL
2/3 cup = 150 mL
3/4 cup = 175 mL
1 cup = 250 mL
2 cups = 1 pint = 500 mL
3 cups = 750 mL
4 cups = 1 quart = 1 L

VOLUME MEASUREMENTS (fluid)

1 fluid ounce (2 tablespoons) = 30 mL
4 fluid ounces (1/2 cup) = 125 mL
8 fluid ounces (1 cup) = 250 mL
12 fluid ounces (1 1/2 cups) = 375 mL
16 fluid ounces (2 cups) = 500 mL

WEIGHTS (mass)

1/2 ounce = 15 g
1 ounce = 30 g
3 ounces = 90 g
4 ounces = 120 g
8 ounces = 225 g
10 ounces = 285 g
12 ounces = 360 g
16 ounces = 1 pound = 450 g

DIMENSIONS

1/16 inch = 2 mm
1/8 inch = 3 mm
1/4 inch = 6 mm
1/2 inch = 1.5 cm
3/4 inch = 2 cm
1 inch = 2.5 cm

OVEN TEMPERATURES

250°F = 120°C
275°F = 140°C
300°F = 150°C
325°F = 160°C
350°F = 180°C
375°F = 190°C
400°F = 200°C
425°F = 220°C
450°F = 230°C

BAKING PAN SIZES

Utensil	Size in Inches/Quarts	Metric Volume	Size in Centimeters
Baking or Cake Pan (square or rectangular)	8×8×2	2 L	20×20×5
	9×9×2	2.5 L	23×23×5
	12×8×2	3 L	30×20×5
	13×9×2	3.5 L	33×23×5
Loaf Pan	8×4×3	1.5 L	20×10×7
	9×5×3	2 L	23×13×7
Round Layer Cake Pan	8×1½	1.2 L	20×4
	9×1½	1.5 L	23×4
Pie Plate	8×1¼	750 mL	20×3
	9×1¼	1 L	23×3
Baking Dish or Casserole	1 quart	1 L	—
	1½ quarts	1.5 L	—
	2 quarts	2 L	—